The Green Book

The Green Book
For Black Folks in Education

Shawn F. Brown

ROWMAN & LITTLEFIELD
Lanham • Boulder • New York • London

Published by Rowman & Littlefield
An imprint of The Rowman & Littlefield Publishing Group, Inc.
4501 Forbes Boulevard, Suite 200, Lanham, Maryland 20706
www.rowman.com

86-90 Paul Street, London EC2A 4NE, United Kingdom

Copyright © 2024 by Shawn F. Brown

All rights reserved. No part of this book may be reproduced in any form or by any electronic or mechanical means, including information storage and retrieval systems, without written permission from the publisher, except by a reviewer who may quote passages in a review.

British Library Cataloguing in Publication Information Available

Library of Congress Cataloging-in-Publication Data Available

ISBN 9781475874051 (cloth) | ISBN 9781475874068 (pbk) | ISBN 9781475874075 (ebook)

If it were not for my relationship with God, I'd have nothing. I give him glory in all that I do. Jennifer, my rock. Your unconditional love and support inspire me to continue dreaming. Junior, Jonathan, and Kaitlyn, I love you beyond what words could describe. To all the students I have had the opportunity to work with, your lives and narratives forced me to write this book. I dedicate this to you. To all my colleagues and staff members, thank you. The work you do matters; you have saved several lives. As Christopher Wallace states, "This goes out to all of the teachers that told me I'd never amount to nothin'." For the haters, I wouldn't be here if it were not for you. Finally, Shaquille and Shaheem. I kept your pictures on my screen saver until this book was done. I hope you are proud.

Contents

Preface	ix
Acknowledgments	xi
Chapter 1: Elementary School	1
Chapter 2: Middle School: *The* Middle Passage	33
Chapter 3: High School	59
References	113

Preface

I was raised in Brownsville, Brooklyn, to a single mother and incarcerated father; according to statistics, my future held two outcomes: jail or six feet under. Living in a community where crime, drugs, and violence saturated the pavement, there were few options. Education became my exit strategy. I was unaware of the cultural norms and systemic biases I would face along that path. Ultimately, with much perseverance, I was able to successfully obtain three masters, advanced certification in Africana studies, and a PhD.

My experiences as a young student have been the driving force behind this book. I aim to use my journey as a road map to guide Black families through the educational school system. There are pragmatic strategies that Black families can use to improve outcomes for their children. This book delivers a step-by-step guide on dealing with the many challenges Black children face while in school.

Historically, the Green Book for Black folks equipped readers for safe passage while traveling throughout the United States. Sundown towns and states that were accepting of Blacks were documented. It saved many lives and taught Black people the importance of being aware of their surroundings when traveling.

Similarly, *The Green Book: For Black Folks in Education* provides the same guidance. Identifying high-quality schools, building relationships with educators, and building community are among the many topics discussed. The systemic issues interwoven in the fabric of education in America is a battle that we continue to fight against. In the interim, I hope this book will serve as a tool to avoid the pitfalls and identify the land mines purposely designed to support agendas that are not in line with the true purpose of education, which is freedom and equality.

Acknowledgments

God, I give you all the glory. Jennifer, you are my rock. Your love inspires me. Shawn Jr., Jonathan, and Kaitlyn, I love you beyond words. To my students, parents, teachers, and colleagues, your lives compelled me to write this book. Mom, thanks for the tough love. Dad, thank you for modeling strength. Dr. Juan Battle, thank you for being authentic, transparent, and unapologetic. Dr. Deborah Shanley, your confidence in me changed my life.

Finally, Shaquille, Shaheem, and Sandro Jr., your pictures remain on my screensaver. Rest peacefully. I hope you are proud.

Chapter 1

Elementary School

The public educational system is a war zone for Black children. History has proved that American educational institutions aren't constructed with Black folks in mind (J. D. Anderson, 1988). The foundation of our educational system is crumbling from the overflow of diversity entering classrooms because it was not created for such demographic/cultural changes. Black babies are in schools designed for entirely different cultures and races. Punishments are more frequent, referrals to special services are higher, resulting in a subconscious disdain for the learning process altogether (Gibson et al., 2014). They are left stranded in facilities that have drained their love for learning yet hold them to the highest standards. The method of draining the joy of learning for Black children starts at an early age.

When entering school buildings, we are unaware of the many trials and tribulations we will face throughout our academic careers. There are rules, codes, and hidden curricula we must follow to have the same experiences of other races (Alsubaie, 2015). These codes are not taught explicitly to us as children. We are subconsciously aware of the rules, but we are never overtly warned of the consequences of choosing not to follow specific social norms. Internally, we have come to accept American education's cultural norms as right, best, and so forth. Conditioning Black children centers on submission, producing docile learners who receive and spew back information. That Black children are silent, submissive, and not heard as students stems from plantation rules for working in the big house. Currently, it is fashionable to speak about the importance of diversity, cultural relevance, systemic racism, and other catchphrases. As with most trends, I wonder how long this trend will last before America finds a new way to segregate and subjugate marginalized folks. Challenging the educational system is reserved for specific people and marginalized folks to an extent. When we challenge the wrong person, we face severe consequences. It's okay to do so among one another in urban school settings, and that is about it. We are treading dangerous waters when we ask why particular schools receive additional funding and demand equitable hiring processes. While we struggle to ask simple questions, others are free to voice anything that comes to mind. The more belligerent and outlandish other races are, the more they are considered mavericks who are "passionate" about education. Give me a break. It is simply a delusion to think that race, class, and gender do not influence one's experience in education (Barnum, 2018). Children of families living in poverty are sitting ducks, unaware of educators' microaggressions.

Educational systems have undetectable caste systems (Wilkerson, 2020). Treatment of children is according to their age, gender, race, and class. The actions of a teenage Black boy and a white female are perceived in different ways. One can identify the unconscious caste system projected onto students based on how teachers interact with students. Teachers are subconsciously training Black children to be factory floor workers who take orders and perform mundane tasks. We are supposed to listen, not speak back, speak but not too loud, look straight ahead but not so straight as to make the teacher feel threatened, ask to use the bathroom but only use it when the teacher says to. Such strict guidelines create an impossible environment for any human being to thrive academically. Children learn more from a teacher's tone, energy, and spirit (which I admit is subjective) than anything else. Regardless of one's disciplinary style, students know their teacher's core values. Educators cannot hide their underlying worldview about the capacities of marginalized children (Young, 2016).

By observing other children's treatment, students quickly learn their place in the educational system's racial hierarchy. Teachers favor some students, while other students are treated harshly. Students then modify their behavior to avoid further abuse. My success as a youngster was my ability to read the temperament of teachers. I knew early on that projecting a subservient demeanor would land me good grades.

On the other hand, I was also well aware of what would happen if I stepped out of line. School was a bed of hot coals on which there was no cool place for us to tread. Most of the time, Black children are figuring out how to deal with educators who are passive aggressive, exhibiting bipolar behavior, or secretly racist, all while solving four-step equations and writing persuasive essays. It's extraordinary meeting Black children who thrive in such disastrous circumstances.

As a student, I would watch teachers all the time. I knew which teachers were serious about their profession. I knew the latecomers perennially rushing in after their start time. Each teacher, whether realizing it or not, made an impression that I still remember. Ms. Wexler was always prepared and ironed her clothes with Niagara Falls spray starch. She was stable emotionally, demanded respect, and challenged my 1st-grade class to excellence. She'd create fun activities that I knew weren't a part of her job description. Then there was a teacher who would bring each problem with her husband into the classroom. While she talked about her Hollywood problems, I was concerned about getting home safe and whether there would be food on the table. A fragrance of despair and stress paced throughout the room as she shared stories about her newborn. Filled with great intentions, I, and I assume most students, was tasked with being a therapist. Thirty-five years later, I recall this teacher as if it were yesterday. The impression that teachers make transcends a lifetime and generations. Whether positive or negative, educators hold a special place in the heart of humanity. When educators disappoint the young, they expose them to a multitude of problems.

Black students turn to alternatives to cope with the trauma they suffer in classrooms. Some purposefully receive out-of-school suspensions, others dull their intellectual capacities to avoid alienation, and still others misbehave, hoping a teacher says they need special services (Toshalis, 2015). A childhood friend would intentionally misbehave to receive SSI (Social Security Income) mental illness benefit checks for groceries. Black children have learned from an oppressive educational system how to find loopholes that serve their needs. Policymakers develop strange definitions such as *at-risk* and the *achievement gap* to justify their positions, and they harm marginalized children. Such policies and unscientific terms further segregate Black students, who receive minimal resources in schools poorly run by unqualified pedagogues. The spin cycle continues without pause, refusing to reconsider strategies that may avoid the usual outcomes.

The Green Book: For Black Folks in Education will clarify the daily confusion that many Black students, parents, and educators feel. In contrast to speaking from a deficit model and holding Black children accountable for the failings of the educational system, this book analyzes the educational system and provides practical solutions. Many Black folks are terrified of school altogether. By examining the beginning of our trauma in schools, we can discover how to navigate the currents of school buildings. Through viewing the experiences of Black people from a different lens, we can learn to function better when faced with challenges. As much as I would like to write about the system of racism that continues to plague our educational system, that rhetoric hasn't gained much traction or led to sweeping policy changes.

Teachers continue harming students and are rarely held accountable for their actions (Kozol, 1985). A security guard chokes/slams a young Black girl and receives desk duty. Leadership selection is based on favoritism and nepotism. Such leaders are unconcerned with transforming the lives of marginalized children. We have spent too much time trying to convince educational systems of their current sins and urging them to repent. I've debated colleagues about racism for hours, and all it did was lead me to fatigue and increased their stubbornness. Black folks have to start training one another on how to survive in the middle of a war. While we march, protest, plead, and beg for change in schools, nothing happens. The weapons of mass destruction are bias policies written to further harm those on the margins. Unbeknownst to Blacks, we have been at war with the educational system since its inception. Trying to convince your enemy to care about and love you makes no sense. Our energies must center on training Black folks to navigate such conditions and improve educational outcomes for our children. We hope that by preparing our families with the tools to navigate the dangerous waters of the educational system, we can help our children improve academically.

BEFORE ENTERING SCHOOL HOME BASE

I was born and raised in Brownsville, Brooklyn. Brownsville is a tightly condensed neighborhood of mostly government housing projects located toward the eastern portion of Brooklyn. I went directly from Brookdale Hospital to Riverdale housing projects. My story isn't much different from many other people from the inner city. As early as I can recall, things were difficult. Both of my parents had migrated from Panama. My dad is from Colon, and my mom is from Panama City. My dad was what one might call a street guy. Unaware of the extent of his involvement, I will leave the rest up to your imagination. With his head bowed in shame, he's confessed to many criminal acts in his earlier years. My mother was a little more conservative in her dealings with people.

While Dad engaged in criminal activities outside the home, Mom took care of my older brother and me. When I was three years old, my dad was arrested and sent to prison for thirteen years. Simultaneously and without realizing it, something snapped internally. My mother recalls me becoming irritable. My aunt Olivia gave me cold baths to calm me down. Before my dad's arrest, he would take me everywhere he went. Even when the situation was hardly safe, he would still have me in tow. Mom said that I made him feel proud. He accomplished something positive in his life of sin. Once he left, though, I did not have the words to articulate what I was feeling. In retrospect, I realize his absence was my first experience with trauma. Before delving deeply through my experiences, I was angry but could discern no reason.

Frequently, young Black children's academic achievement is negatively impacted by dysfunctional parent modeling and involvement (Wilder, 2014). I struggled academically as a result of my dad's incarceration, a mother raising three boys, an impoverished community, and an Americanized school system. Like me, many of our Black students reside in homes with single parents. Black women independently lead most Black homes. Black mothers are strong, resilient, reliable—but they don't always want to be. My mother had to carry the stress of raising three Black boys in the middle of the most dangerous communities in New York City. As I entered school, my teachers had no clue of the inner turmoil brewing in me.

For educators welcoming young children for the first time, take a moment to pause. Before getting through a curriculum, focus on building meaningful relationships (Bidwell & Stinson, 2016). Stop and think about some of the challenges that you are about to encounter. You'll have children entering school for the first time who have gone through more in their five years of existence than most adults in their lifetimes. Many of these students have been physically, verbally, and sexually abused. Others are raised by emotionally available parents. Many Black children come from amazing households and aren't prepared for the visceral hatred that people have toward them because of their skin tone. These little scholars may not know how to verbalize the inner tensions from factors mentioned earlier, but you can see the fruits of these issues in their body language, tone, lack of eye contact, and so forth. Educators must develop the ability to see early signs and address issues immediately. The best way is to have transparent conversations with parents.

Kindergarten

Going to school is a memorable experience for children. This is the first time that many of them are away from their parents for an extended time. Many have a hard time transitioning. Their comfort level depends on their personality and understanding of social norms before entering a school building. School transitions are incredibly different for Black children.

Recently, I had the opportunity to witness this special occasion with my youngest daughter (Kaitlyn) as she started kindergarten. The first day she was beyond excited. She had trouble sleeping the night before. Being a social butterfly, she enjoyed meeting new friends. Parents were allowed to walk them into their class and set up their desks. Her class was located on the first floor, close to the back door entrance. As parents, my wife and I were super nervous about her attending school. Our fear stemmed more from our experiences in schools and what we had heard from others.

For many Black parents, there are mixed emotions on that first day. We would have loved the comfort of knowing that our babies would be treated with love when we weren't around. However, the constant videos of Black children's abuse in classrooms did not allow us to drop our guard. We frantically warned our children to tell us everything that was going on in the classroom. Our children's ability to articulate their experiences is a crucial skill when they are in school. In many schools, Black children are told not to tell parents about incidents that happen in school. When such orders come from adults, children become confused. There are mixed messages from parents and educators. For example, adults tell children to remain silent, fold their hands, raise their hand before speaking, and never talk back to a teacher. Such directives from adults cause children to disengage from learning. Being a student becomes too complicated and tiresome. From the outside, educators who are this strict with Black students seem firm, organized, structured, and disciplined. A deeper dive into such discipline reveals a desire to train children from an early age to know their place, not only in classrooms but in society (Ferguson, 2001). Black parents naively reason that if children are "well behaved," they'll be treated with kindness. This falsity also encourages Black parents to punish further, physically, and verbally abuse children when teachers claim they are "disruptive" in class. Too many times, we are sadly mistaken about the level of harm inflicted on our children. Students who can adhere to overt messages of the importance of submission become incapable of developing self-confidence as scholars.

As I have stated, I was born and raised in Brownsville, Brooklyn—one of the most densely populated communities in the United States—in the late 1970s and started school in the 1980s (Meminger, 2020). The period of the Reagan administration ushered in the influx of crack cocaine. An epidemic was raging in most minority-populated inner-city communities. Violence became a primary mode of communication in my area. While going to bed, I conditioned myself to sleep through shootouts. Even as a kindergartener, I had been socialized to consider such violence as standard. Most of the conflict was between warring neighboring housing projects. I lived in the Riverdale Houses, which are across the street from the Tilden Houses. Crossing Livonia Avenue at the Rockaway train station could mean the end of your life. Teachers who worked in such communities had no clue what was happening after the last bell rang and students walked home.

Educators must learn the socioeconomic landscape Black children have to navigate before entering a school. Unfortunately, some educators do not believe it is a part of their job description to understand the nuances of a child's life outside of the classroom. Along with socioeconomic and community hardships, conflicts between their parents influence students. On several occasions, I have seen parents have verbal altercations in front of their children. Hostile exchanges between parents transfer over into their children's performance in school. The process of learning demands a safe environment before entering school.

Near my housing projects, there is a kindergarten right next to the train stations. It lies in between Riverdale and Tilden Houses. It serves all of the prekindergarten and kindergarten children in the community. My older brother Michael walked me to school before going off to PS 41 with my cousin Jamilah. We all lived at 365 Thatford Avenue and traveled everywhere together during our childhood. Siblings and cousins going to school together was not just a convenience but a form of protection. If you had no siblings or relatives, you would walk to school with people from your housing projects, starting in kindergarten. Kindergarten was filled with fun and adventure. There were floor spots, name tags, nap time, and a host of chores that made you feel like an adult. Our teachers were loving and kind and reminded me of my mom, aunt, and grandmother. During recess, we would run and scream until our voices gave out. Freeze tag, flies up, handball, skelly, and a list of old 1970s games were always on the menu. Nap time for an hour always followed recess. This stage of education is a blur for most people of all races. I am not sure if it was trauma or some weird self-defense mechanism that I developed, but I sincerely don't remember negative things happening in school. The educational system and Black communities were different then. My feelings were less affected by what was happening in the school building than by issues in the neighborhood. My trauma, at approximately three years old, came from my father's incarceration (Parke & Clarke-Stewart, 2002).

My dad emigrated from Panama and got himself into trouble when he came to America. I am not sure when he arrived in the US. From what I gather, he started working at local grocery stores, making an honest living. Eventually, the money was not coming fast enough. Lured into criminality, he started selling drugs and robbing people coming from the local train station. He looked like a mixed-race kid with an honest face. One evening the opportunity to rob a real estate company came up. It was supposed to be an easy task. In and out with no problems. As with most crimes, nothing goes as planned. Long story short, there was some sort of shooting, and my father got hit. He ran, hid under a parked car along the street, trying to hide. He was unaware of an older woman watching from her second-story window. An older white woman saw him hiding and alerted the police. Armed robbery resulted in a five-to-seven-year sentence. Altercations while in prison, coupled with his original sentence, eventually led to a thirteen-year bid. I was three years old, and my dad was gone. This event informed the way I entered into school, even in kindergarten.

As teachers welcome young Black babies into their classrooms for the first time, they must consider what walks in with them. Droves of children have absent parents, Black fathers in particular. Whether through tensions between parents or fathers feeling unable to be what their children need, the truth is that many dads aren't in their children's lives. Parental absence leads to internal conflicts that children wrestle with for a lifetime. Research indicates that incarceration weakens the bonds between parents and their children, creating insecure attachment, decreased cognitive abilities, and weak peer relationships (Parke & Clarke-Stewart, 2002). As a student, I was angry all the time. Later I realized that my hero was gone, and anger seemed like the best way to express my emotions.

Feelings of absence came in waves while in school. I'd frequently go into my dad's closet to wear his sheepskin and applejack hat. At this age, he was a mystery. I would daydream about him walking me to school and taking me from the housing projects to the park. My mom tells me that I started being very aggressive and angry all the time. Spiritually, I believe kids know what is happening, even when they don't know what is happening. Children have a purity of heart that gives them the ability to sense things better than adults. Older individuals develop self-defense mechanisms, and coping mechanisms to deal with trauma. Young people, not yet capable of using such filters, are more sensitive to the actions of adults.

I can recall visiting my dad when I was young. He was in prison, but I thought it was a fun trip to see my dad. When I became older, I realized what had happened. The rage grew stronger over time as I realized that he would never get on the bus home after leaving Rikers Island. For students entering schools, as early as ages four to five, they have developed a sense of their environment that makes them defensive, aggressive, and so forth. Educators and parents cannot personalize incidents when children are simply expressing frustration regarding a deeper problem.

Some educators have a hard time relating to stories of hurt and loss because they've never experienced it firsthand. Everyone has experienced hurt and loss, but it is different based on one's race, class, gender, and socioeconomic status. For example, for a person losing a parent, it's painful regardless of their race. When a Black child loses a father or mother, they have very little resources in their extended family to replace such a great loss. Other races, other ethnicities have family and community members who have resources. Most Black families do not. Furthermore, several educators do not believe it is their responsibility to learn about these aspects of their students' lives. Too often, they believe the child's misbehavior indicates needing special education services. Teachers immediately think that harsh rules, regulations, and rigid structures are the best way to get children to comply. Their lack of empathy is viewed as a strength in the school community. Teachers are subconsciously permitted to be as harsh as they please without any consequences. Such teachers lack the social-emotional skills to teach children without resorting to abuse. Enabling teachers to abuse students starts with uninvolved parents with blind trust in the school system.

Guidance for Parents curing Kindergarten

Parents can help their children transition into a new life phase when they begin school. How Black children transition into school is primarily based on how their parents prepare them. Black parents/guardians must have transparent conversations with their children about the realities of racism. In the Black community, such dialogue comes primarily from Black mothers. Statistics indicate that Black females lead most Black households (Jackson, 1999). Many Black parents eventually divorce or never marry. Generations of children are reared in homes with one parent making all decisions. Taking a Black kid to kindergarten is traumatizing yet relieving at the same time. The danger is that some parents send their children to school without communicating with school personnel. Drained from working, supporting multiple children, and trying to have their own social life, single parents struggle to dialogue with educators consistently.

Carmen Brown, my mother, made sure that every person in our school understood the consequences of mistreating her children. She'd never yell or scream at the teacher; that was not her way. Instead, she would have professional conversations about her concerns and made sure to follow up. Her methods were not popular. During that time, most parents blindly followed the teacher's advice without question. Also, she held my brother and me to high expectations as students. My brother and I were taught to be respectful, do our work, and avoid trouble, a form of discipline that parents may have embraced in past generations, but we are in different times.

Along with holding students to high standards of excellence, we must also hold teachers to the same standards. Successful schools require quality leadership and effective instructors in our classrooms (Gill & Lerner, 2017). High-quality, culturally relevant instruction is no longer optional for Black children but a necessity. It is not as if racism and abuse didn't happen in the past. Presently, the abuse is harder to detect. Our babies are encountering teachers who, at their core, have a distinct loathing for children. It is not wise to send children into an educational facility, even kindergarten, without giving them the language they need to articulate when they're mistreated. My mother was straightforward with us on how to share our emotions, thoughts, and concerns. It was her only way to help us if we were in trouble. She regularly questioned us about how school was going and taught us how to study teachers. I forgot what grade I was in when a teacher tried to harm my older brother. From what I recall, he hit my other brother or said something hurtful. That wasn't good for the teacher. My mother proceeded to go to the school and give that teacher a verbal lashing he'd never forget. In this instance, my mother made an exception because she realized that the teacher was in the wrong. Even in this instance, if the teacher had admitted fault, my mother would have been calm. The teacher's attitude, tone, and arrogance unleashed hell on earth. Being a Black woman from a low-income community, she was always cognizant of her presentation. She never wanted to be seen as the typical *Angry Black Woman*. In that moment, she felt compelled by a sense of desperation. Parents struggle at times to defend their children when there is turmoil in the home. The breakdown between mothers and fathers leaves our children even more vulnerable when in school. To rectify this, we must clarify each parent's roles when interacting with their children's school.

Many Black men believe handling school business for their children is a female's job. Others are absent quite often and become ashamed when trying to be better. Then some have grown weary of awkward stares and backhanded compliments (Neal, 2018). Growing up in a single-parent household, I thought parent-teacher meetings were supposed to be attended only by mothers. My father's absence, coupled with a misogynistic viewpoint constructed from intentional socialization in a Eurocentric society, caused me to devalue his influence. For active fathers wanting to be involved in their child's education, few teachers look like us. Reports indicate that the educational system's teaching force is 80 percent white female teachers (Loewus, 2017). From our personal experiences as Black men, going into a school building for any reason is traumatic. Our trauma comes in many forms due to our experiences as students. When attempting to do well in school, many have been teased, beat up, and alienated. The "nerd" who hears he is *corny* has as many psychological scars as a *thug* placed improperly in special education. Many of us lost our innocence as children in school—innocence in terms of how we viewed the world. Before school, we were naïve. I thought racism wasn't that bad, that I could make mistakes like normal kids and be forgiven. False labels of learning disabled have left generations of Black men terrified of education in its totality. When I speak with older men about the possibility of returning to finish school, a similar theme arises. "Nah, man, it just ain't for me." "I don't know; I never liked school, to be honest." Though they cannot pinpoint the exact reason, I confidently assume that it started at the beginning of their educational journey. A teacher's harshness, a bad grade, their parents not advocating for them, and so on.

Black parents wrestle with recognizing best parental practices for their children when it comes to school. We tend to go to varying extremes. Some choose to avoid our children's schools; others become overly aggressive. We ask ourselves, "Do I curse this teacher out for giving my child an undeserved grade, or do I act professionally and yell at my child?" Many of us do the latter, thinking that verbally abusing our children in front of teachers is "professional." This thinking stems from strategies used to protect Black children during slavery. The theory was that a parent should abuse, misuse, and embarrass the child so much so that slavers could not do even worse. Slavery in the United States was unlike any other instance of human enslavement in terms of scale, duration, and consequences (Leary, 2004). Showing too much kindness to your child at the time could lead to death. We developed extreme defense mechanisms out of fear for our babies. Because of these negative interactions, we subconsciously stay away from being present in educational settings. We don't realize that absence is the worst message to give to an educator. Teachers start to feel more comfortable abusing your child, knowing there will be no repercussions. From personal experience, I have to contact my children's teachers when I notice that their tone and attitude is getting too familiar with my children. No matter how many degrees or titles I earn, being present trumps them all. Parents, especially fathers, have to communicate with teachers; it is our job. Many parents have struggles that we feel ashamed to disclose. If you, as a parent, dropped out of school, have a learning disability, or have difficulty with the English language, speaking with teachers is a nightmare. Imagine being unable to help your child understand their work. Going into a kindergarten class can feel like torture for many of us. I've seen many fathers drop their kids at school, deliver their lunch, and pay for school events without ever stepping foot in the school building. It's like kryptonite. There are many solutions to this problem. Being present doesn't mean being perfect. Your presence alone is all that is needed. Be clear about your goals and expectations for your child.

Black parents must be publicly affectionate to their children, especially in the presence of educators (Thomas, 2017). By your actions, educators understand they cannot harm your baby without accountability. I remember having a parent conference with an ex-felon and his son. His son had chosen to join a gang as a freshman. The dad had just gotten out of prison a few months earlier. Now he wanted to dedicate his life to steering his son in the right direction. The student's father stood six foot three and weighed approximately 250 pounds. He had tattoo tears and what looked like war scars on his hands. I informed him of his son's bad grades and gang initiation. His father began to cry and begged his son to stop. The father, with bloodshot eyes, looked at me and said, "I love my son, and I am willing to die for him at any moment." He solved no mathematic equation; he did not complete a thirty-page essay. In that one statement, he made it clear that I, as an administrator, had better do right by his son. His presence and that statement informed me of who I needed to be for his son at all times.

Throughout my professional career, asking to speak with the father of a child seems disrespectful. There is a sense of embarrassment or anger that covers the face of most mothers. "He is not present" is the common response. I am not sure if that means the father has passed, remains incarcerated, or is disinterested. To avoid further tension, I stop asking questions. Once I bring up the father, the mood changes. The student becomes stoic, the mother usually seems emotional. As a son, I have been in conferences such as these. When teachers would ask about my dad, my mind might float away. Unable to deal with the pain, I envisioned playing ball with friends, or watching *Alvin and the Chipmunks*. Anything to avoid reality. As an educator, I can recall several situations when asking to communicate with the father led to emotional responses from parents and students. Contrary to the media's portrayal of Black men, they desire to teach their children alternatives to harmful practices (Threlfall et al., 2013). I have seen Black fathers, when given the opportunity, support their child's growth in astounding ways. A few years back, there was a student who continued to get in trouble. He cut class, got into arguments with teachers, and frequently was suspended. We tried speaking with guidance counselors, basketball coaches, and every person who could help. Finally, I pulled the youngster into my office and sat him down with one of our school's deans. I kept asking what the problem was. Why was he so angry? He eventually shared something that has become all too familiar—the broken heart of a kid crying out for his dad. His behavior is an outward manifestation of the "hurt" left in the wake of a father's absence. But, unfortunately, the so-often deeply buried emotional pain—and for some boys their mental health problems—are not getting the attention required to help them heal and be made whole (Joiner, 2016). Now, his father was not a bad guy. He was still in the kid's life. The father simply refused to come to the school and check in with his kid. Even if he did something good, Dad wasn't there. To be fair, he was a very busy blue-collar construction worker. He made it very clear that he did not mind talking with his son about being better, but he did not want to come to the school under any circumstance. As an old-school Caribbean guy, he didn't care to sit down and talk with teachers. He didn't see the point. Whether he was right or wrong is not the point. Educators and mothers need to know that Black men have reasons not to want to be around schools. I do not justify such behavior, but to improve communication, we must understand the underlying trepidation. Because there are so few Black men involved in school, those in two-parent homes must share our resources with those who lack such resources.

Black families with both parents cannot afford to be merely self-serving in addressing what needs to be done to help Black children in schools. We cannot be only concerned with what is happening with our children and nothing else. That way of thinking is selfish and not in alignment with African tradition. People substitute absent extended families with members of the same ethnic or national community who fulfill the family's role at home in the African tradition. Members of the community can offer advice to young people, resolve family disputes, provide moral and financial assistance in times of crisis or death, and celebrate happy events such as weddings and births (Martin & Mitchell, 1982). Conversely, African Americans adhere to Westernized isolated, competitive family practices. The world could be falling apart, and as long as our kids are well, nothing else matters. Such egocentric thinking has led to many of our young ones being abandoned. Many of us have reached a certain level of success, and we do not want to get distracted by anyone else's problems. I have to remember that advocating for other people's children is nonnegotiable. Reaching out to support other families hasn't gone well for some of us; therefore, some have stopped trying altogether. We cannot allow one bad moment to change our core values. We also do not want our children to be influenced negatively by other children. Therefore, we isolate and cut off all ties to any person who can even come close to negatively impacting our children. Such isolation is fool's gold and eventually becomes harmful. Overly sheltering our children leaves them vulnerable when they are older. There are numerous reasons that successful Black families believe extreme isolation is the best way to raise children. First, low-income Black families that have struggled to make it to the middle class are terrified of going back. Any semblance of that environment causes extreme anxiety. Second, Black middle-class success has a toxic competitive component. Isolation is a form of staying ahead of others, those whom one perceives as competition. Through conditioning we have been trained to see each other as enemies. Next, we follow the behaviors of others who have been successful. Our sense of success is measured by and based on the strategies that have worked for other races. Other races seem to have done well by isolating themselves from Blacks; thus, we imitate their behaviors.

Then some families are desperate to keep their elite status within white communities. We have worked hard to finally strip away all semblance of our Blackness to be accepted into elitist groups. Skin bleaching, European hair wigs, and speech modifications to fit the status quo are a path for several Black elitists. Colorism and passing as white have divided the Black community for centuries. The divide in skin tone impacts the finances of families in the Black community. Colorism shows up in even starker ways: the difference in pay rates between darker-skinned and lighter-skinned men mirrors the differences in pay between whites and Blacks (Greenidge, 2019). The difference in salaries impacts Black families' ability to purchase homes, start a business, or pursue generational wealth. Like crabs in a barrel, we compete against one another for the few available prominent positions at work and in the community. The thought of engaging another Black person in these environments becomes detrimental to our advancement. We are big fish in a small pond. Some of us have put ourselves in the financial position of never having to interact with lower-class Black folks. We maintain a conservative posture at all times, attending to all white rules that go along with sitting at the "cool" table. We down-talk our people, laugh harder than required, and even suffer embarrassment to ensure that our legacies continue to transition.

Recently, I moved to a middle-class town after being in Brooklyn my entire life. The change in zip code was also a cultural shift for my family and me. In Brooklyn, there were always Black folks that leaned toward an elitist profile. On the other hand, some Black communities remain proud and unconcerned with adhering to European social norms. When coming to this community, I realized that the latter group was small to nonexistent, while the former group was the overwhelming majority. As proud of her Blackness as anyone on this earth, my wife suggested a Black history celebration at a school meeting. The suggestion was taken with a grain of salt and subtly pushed to the side.

Jennifer (my wife) is simply not the one to cordially ignore. She has a sixth sense when being disregarded. Also, her community organization skills are next level. She began organizing a group, planning events, speaking with local vendors, arranging food, and so forth. We then had our first celebration and forever changed what celebrating Blackness looks like in our community. What was of interest is all the Black folks who secretly said, "Sister, it is about time that someone did something." My question was, "Why did it take all this time, and why did a new community member lead it?" Quick answer: fear. Middle-class Black folks can sometimes act like they just made it into the big house on the plantation. We (Black people) must move away from separatist views of one another based on class, skin tone, and other peripheral labels that only distract us.

Black people must develop healthy friendships with people in our children's schools. Development of social capital must commence in kindergarten (Hunter et al., 2019). When entering a new school, start from a place of positivity. Your child's teacher needs to be the first person you build a bridge with. First, introduce yourself at the start of the year. See what supplies are needed. Ask about the teacher's pet peeves, teaching history, favorite subjects, and the like. Get to know them outside of the school setting. Next, speak with other teachers. Notice how other staff members react when you mention a teacher's name. Staff members cannot hide their energy and know which teachers are dangerous. Third, read body language. Does the teacher look at you in your eyes? Do they speak over you? Do they smile often? Subtle behaviors tell you a lot about their personality. They can be your child's most crucial advocate or worst nightmare. Exchange phone numbers, see if there are any supplies needed for the class, communicate regularly. Set aside to volunteer in the school if you can. Let the teacher know that you are allies and not enemies.

But what are Black parents hearing? We are wondering, should we have to do all of this just to get decent service from our child's teacher? Yes, we should. But we have to be honest with ourselves about how the educational system works. Each year my wife and I are adamant about purchasing needed supplies for our children's teachers. We remember their birthdays, special events, and we usually end the year off with a gift card. There are a couple of reasons we do this.

First and foremost, we try to be generous to everyone we cross in the school building. School aides, security, janitors, and principals, we believe in treating all kindly. Second, our most precious investments will be in the facility for six to eight hours daily. I want the people around them to know me well and think twice before harming my babies. I am fully aware of how Black children are treated when their parents do not have the best relationships with staff members. Each day those little children have to deal with microaggressions from staff based on their parents' actions. I've seen teachers hold grudges toward students for years, cajole other staff members into holding a grudge, and impede students' progress academically. It sounds ridiculous, but it happens more than you may think. As a principal, there were many times I had to put my ego aside and ask what my real issue with the student was. Many times, veteran staff members have called me on the carpet and forced me toward the mirror.

Developing a healthy rapport with staff members who dislike you and your child is difficult. Black parents are okay with strategies, theories, and considering findings from articles. But once a staff member is blatantly disrespectful, all bets are off. Titles, degrees, and years of seniority are of no value when choosing to be rude toward parents. As an educator, I was once told by a parent, "Please do not come for me if I did not send for you." Parents have checked my dismissive, belittling tone when speaking to them. I recall having a thirty-minute-long parents conference with two parents. I had a decent discussion with the mom, and the meeting was coming to an end. As the meeting began to wrap up, the father stated, "You never once looked at me or asked me a single question." He then left after I begged him to share his insight. The damage was done, and my message of how much I valued his thoughts was clear. Educators can be disrespectful as a result of wanted to *move on* to the next thing. Parents are great at detecting when someone devalues them early. The subtle smile, handshake, tone, lack of eye contact are all signs. Parents pick up nuanced microaggressions from teachers from the first time they meet. Sometimes it is just our insecurities—other times, it's intuition (Spidey senses). My advice for parents is to be firm and professional. You may see a teacher's actions worthy of a good tongue lashing; consider the repercussions your child may face. For cases of abuse, by all means, fully verbalize your emotions. Additionally, consider taking your child out of the class and school. Some situations call for a community of parental support. When is that support necessary? What is it likely to look like? How do we encourage the community building? To these issues we turn next.

COLLABORATIVE PARENTING

When first taking your babies into schools, speak to veteran parents who have already been through the educational system. Our strength is and has always been our ability to work collaboratively. Unfortunately, that sense of togetherness has dissipated over the years. We are victims of systemic racism.

Divisive, toxic competitiveness is sewn into our subconscious. Intentionally socialized to have interracial tensions, we have trouble developing healthy relationships with other parents. We can be in large crowds, all picking up our children simultaneously, and not say a word to one another. There are profound historical implications for this behavior. Blacks were first purposefully separate to avoid slave revolts. Tulsa and Seneca Village, among many other united Black communities, were targeted throughout the U.S. Economically independent, thriving Black communities were purposefully flooded or removed for lakes and parks. The trend, starting in the early 1910s and lasting over several decades, was carried out through racial violence, intimidation, and discriminatory legal practices (Smith, 2021). Black Panthers, Malcolm X, and Martin Luther King Jr. received the same treatment every time we have tried to unite as a race. The result is a race of people perpetually at odds with one another without ever comprehensively examining the root causes. Parents have fistfights in front of schools over social media gossip. We win small wars against one another while losing the battle of protecting our children. What someone says, who they are dating, or what misinterpreted *shade* a person throws cannot remain our focus. Periodically, in church, a portion of the service calls members to greet their neighbors. As a race, we must do the same. Embrace one another as friends, colleagues, brothers, and sisters. Once the conversation starts, our similarities become unmistakable. To clarify the point, we do not have to be best friends. Being cordial and resolving conflicts without resorting to violence is a good start. When Black folks do not display a sense of solidarity, a message transmits to those educating our children.

I have had to come in between parents prepared to kill one another over a slight miscommunication. Once a girl had gotten into a conflict with another student. I first spoke to both students, contacted their parents, and set up a conference to resolve the dispute. Something negative was said in a social media post. A boyfriend was the center of the problem for the two young ladies. Text messages, social media posts, and gossip turned into threats. Gangs and deadly weapons were discussed as one of the girls proceeded to call her family. Her family was notorious throughout Bushwick, Brooklyn. Known for gang affiliation and prepared to do anything to protect the little girl, they pulled up to the school in a couple of cars. Her dad was in prison for some serious charges but still had street power. Her uncles and cousins assumed the role of protector. When three o'clock came around, I stepped out to conduct dismissal for all the students. There were minivans and jeeps outside as students were walking home. What made the situation most intense was the *abuela* (grandmother). The student's grandmother stood all but four feet tall, one hundred pounds, lightly colored grays, and cursed with an old-school Spanish accent. Most of the threats came from her. The uncles lay waiting on word from the grandma. Standing in disbelief with the security guard, I was confused. I asked myself, "Will I have to call the police on Grandma?" We sometimes take conflicts to the furthest extent, even when it is not necessary. To be clear, other racial groups have similar disagreements. The idea of *Black on Black* crime is propaganda. At the same time, there is much to learn about how different groups address their problems with one another.

When traveling, I see other ethnicities that don't even know each other hugging and going to the local restaurants in airports for a bite to eat. While working with colleagues of different races, I notice that their conflicts are settled in private or simply not discussed at all. Other races can be publicly violent with one another, too. However, from my experience, I think we (Black people) should be a bit more discreet when airing out grievances. I remember two teachers who hated one another. They stayed away from one another and never spoke negatively about the other to anyone in school. What is the difference? There is a sense of solidarity, friendship, and goodwill. There is a comfort in being violent toward our own that we must stop. As parents, we have to develop Black solidarity for the sake of our children, if not for each other. Having that mindset is still a challenge for many. There are historical reasons for such animosity toward each other.

History documents the stealing of Blacks and how they were intentionally divided against one another for our slavers to maintain control. Starting with Jamestown in 1619 through to the civil rights era, the continued oppression of Black people centers on destabilizing our unity. Blacks are abused in legal systems, the medical field, and especially in schools (Bell, 1993; Ladson-Billings, 2007). Facing such opposition, having tensions toward one another is absurd. We cause self-inflicted scars when we wage war against each other. Blacks cannot afford dissension based on skin tone, class, sexual identity, or other frivolous categories. Most schools have support staff (custodians, security, teacher aides) that are, for the most part, Black and Latino. From my experience in schools, such individuals have a pulse on the school community. Rarely, however, do teachers or administrators fully understand the deeper cultural context of a school. The support staff members are underutilized resources that Black families must engage more often.

Support Staff

Paraprofessionals, bus drivers, custodians, and secretaries are vital support staff for the school community. It's important that we acknowledge the work that they do and ensure they have the resources and respect they deserve (Kukuk, 2019). Healthy relationships between support staff, teachers, and parents ensure student success. You don't have to be best friends with a teacher who does not like you. Many educators could not care less about your struggles and problems, to be honest. The truth is that teachers did not sign up for that kind of drama. As you visit the school, take a look into the cafeteria, strike up a conversation with the security guard, use the bathroom, and try to run into the janitor in the hallway. These are the unsung heroes who will protect your child when no one else will.

Some of my closest friends/advisors are the security guards, custodians, and cafeteria staff. Once there were rumors of a teacher secretly mistreating students and abusing pharmaceutical drugs on the job. I had been having issues with this staff member for a couple of years. His behavior was erratic and inconsistent for some time. I had documented every exchange with this teacher. The staff member came to work late, unprepared, and smelled unsanitary. I provided professional development and encouraged other staff to intervene. We spoke about personal issues that were happening at home. I called his union representative to try to help. My efforts, along with the staff, did not lead to changed behavior. The final straw was when he chose to leave the building without permission and with a room full of students in a classroom. Educational neglect is a serious offense that despite my compassion I couldn't ignore. I went to the room, and the staff member was walking out, ready to leave. The person stared at me with a certain aggression that reminded me of my old community. You see, when you look another person, especially a Black man, in the eye, like you want to get physical, it sets off an alert. Against my better judgment, I asked, "What are you trying to do?" You see, at this point, I was willing to lose my job before letting another human feel comfortable trying to intimidate me. A veteran science teacher saw what was about to happen and stood in between us. My pounding heart interrupted my speech. Combinations ran rampant in my mind. Left, right, hook, pull, jab, et cetera.

I also considered the possibility of the person having a firearm. I told one of our support staff members about what had happened. To my surprise, I was informed that the person regularly hid alcohol in his coffee mug. I took formal statements about this staff member. The investigation led to the removal of the staff member from the building. The sad part was the person was merely transferred to a different school. Without help from the support staff member, his abuse could have led to something more dangerous. As an administrator, I hold my support staff in high regard. I have a team of support staff members who can connect with students whom most refuse to engage. Black families must use support staff members as eyes and ears if they cannot connect with teachers.

Black and Brown folks usually maintain school support positions in their community. Building relationships with support staff may come more naturally than with teachers for Black parents. Experiential knowledge from such staff members is priceless. They choose not to say much to instructional staff. Their suggestions are pushed aside. These individuals have a heightened level of social intellect when it comes to students and teachers. If your child is struggling, they can tell you with near-perfect accuracy. For example, our cafeteria lady often stops after-school fights before they even start. She fades into the background, clearing food trays while listening to the daily gossip. Listen to their words and take heed to their advice, for they hold the key to ensuring that your child is safe and in a nurturing environment. Of these support staff members, no one is more aware of what is happening in the classrooms than the paraprofessionals.

Paraprofessionals

Paraprofessionals are support staff members who work with special-needs students. The students' diagnoses range from emotionally disturbed to learning disabled. Assignments vary based on the needs of the students. Some are crisis interventionists; others are classroom assistants. Throughout my career, I have had the privilege of working with some beautiful paraprofessionals. I'd be remiss not to share my first experience of working with a fantastic paraprofessional.

When I first became a teacher, my assignment was in elementary school. I first taught in a coteaching situation with a special education instructor and eventually took over a self-contained classroom. Self-contained classrooms usually hold approximately twelve special education students and a paraprofessional for support. A colleague had recently graduated from the Teaching Fellows program in New York City and was having difficulty. He'd come from Africa by way of Minnesota. Unprepared for the cultural shifts in working with students from New York City, he began to sink into a toxic place psychologically. I took over his class, allowing him to work with my veteran collaborative teacher; as a result, he would be less stressed working with a veteran. I moved from the second to the third floor: one teacher, one paraprofessional, and twelve students. Unbeknownst to me, this paraprofessional became my guardian angel.

When I began teaching, my paraprofessional was an older Black woman, religious and filled with grace. She frequently shared positive words of wisdom. She reminded me of Clair Huxtable. Classy, firm, yet gentle, and even forceful when necessary. Truthfully, she ran that classroom better than I could. She remembered everyone's birthday. No matter how small the gesture, each student felt like royalty when she was present. Before BlackBerrys and iPhones, she kept me on track. Grading papers, writing lesson plans, and updating bulletin boards were done promptly because of her. During this portion of my career, I had my first child and was completing work for my master's program at Brooklyn College. I'd work from eight in the morning to three in the afternoon. Next, I would ride a broken-down bike—given to me as a gift from home—to class at Brooklyn College. Averaging four hours of sleep, I would often doze off while sitting at my desk. She would give me a nudge and tell me to wash my face in the bathroom. While walking back in, she would be giving students handouts and running the class. Words such as "grateful" and "appreciative" wouldn't fully explain my sentiments. Educators and administrators would do well to bring such people into conversations about what is best for children. When hiring new staff, we should consider leadership strategies, instructional focus, and, most importantly, how we engage students. Educators may disregard paraprofessionals because they lack distinct academic credentials. Their experience must be held in higher regard. Some may not have finished school for personal reasons. However, the lack of a degree shouldn't take away from their insights and perspectives. Having a hierarchical mentality stops educators from listening to paraprofessionals.

Paraprofessionals are subconsciously told that they are to be seen and not heard. Within the Department of Education, people respect titles more than experience. A person could be in a school for three decades, but they are looked down upon if they do not have a specific title or college degree. This Americanized way of valuing people based on hierarchy stops school communities from supporting students comprehensively. Support staff members become discouraged, knowing their ideas aren't honored. Some burn out and quit, while others stay quiet while students aren't appropriately serviced.

I humbly admit to previously having a top-down leadership attitude. I came into a school of primarily veteran staff. My supervisor placed me in charge of the special education department. I was responsible for all special education students having updated individual educational plans (IEPs). Those of us in education know that these are legal documents. If taken care of improperly, a person can lose their career. I tried my best to organize these files and ensure that they were up to date. No matter how hard I tried, I couldn't get it done the right way. After struggling on my own, I asked my supervisor for an assistant. A veteran paraprofessional reached out to help. Once again, support staff see problems a mile away. She was of Haitian descent, with a work ethic that was second to none. While she was considering supporting my efforts, I subconsciously was thinking, what is the catch? "What does she want in exchange for helping me?" I thought quietly. Such thinking is the result of excessive insecurity and a lack of leadership training. I was projecting my way of thinking. I thought, "People aren't genuinely kind without wanting a favor." How arrogant and prideful of me! But this is the mindset of several educators when it comes to their relationships with paraprofessionals. The paraprofessionals I have met are sincere and care little about praise. Their hard work is done silently, with pure intentions. Utilize them and also treat them with respect as human beings.

Over the years, I have realized that support staff members are the heart of every school community. They can flourish in their roles and even consider obtaining additional degrees to teach within a school community if given support. Currently, I have teachers who were paraprofessionals and security agents. All they needed was a little push and a few words of encouragement. As leaders, we have to be willing to humble ourselves and seek their support when needed. School staff are amazing advocates and the best persons to inform a parent about what is happening with their children.

Listen to Your Child

One day in elementary school, my older brother came home crying. He stated that a teacher yelled at him or hit him. I do not recall precisely what happened. Either way, he was distraught. My brother rarely got into trouble when in school. He was and still is an introvert. My mother was extremely concerned as he rarely caused problems. If it were me, she would have thought otherwise because I was notorious for clowning around. She always had to interrogate me before approaching a teacher. But my brother was different. He explained to me that his teacher did something wrong to him. My mother's rule was to respect those in authority until they blatantly disrespected you. Not just on this occasion, but there were times that my mother had a few choice words for teachers. I share this story to discuss the importance of having an open line of communication with your children.

Parents developing healthy listening skills can save their children's lives. Active listening entails being interested and attentive, encouraging conversation, listening patiently, hearing children out, and paying attention to nonverbal cues. As parents learn to listen, their children's listening skills improve in school (Smith, 1993). As parents, we tend to dismiss our children when they share their thoughts, feelings, and emotions. More important than their words, we have to read their nonverbal expressions. Approximately 85 percent of communication is nonverbal. When our children transition to kindergarten, barely able to speak as it is, they express feelings in alternative ways. Parents must listen with a distinct ear when children return home. A debriefing must be happening every day that your child comes home from school. Search their bodies for strange markings, scars, and so forth. Be a student of their patterns and tendencies. If your child usually takes a nap when they come home and then wants to go and play for hours one day, something could be wrong. This sudden burst of energy, though seemingly innocent, may be a cry for help. Don't assume everything is all right. It may not be. The most significant change you may notice is eye contact. Some of our children start kindergarten assertive, articulate, and bold. After a few weeks, they are mumbling, looking to the ground, and afraid to share what they are thinking. These behaviors can be the result of abusive language from staff members, disguised as tough love. If this is the case, your child is in danger and desperately needs you to protect them.

In the past, parents could, to some extent, trust their child's teacher. Daily videos of teachers committing brutal crimes against Black children have taken that luxury away. I'm still traumatized from watching videos online of Black babies getting beaten by a security guard, being cursed out by teachers, and experiencing sexual harassment (N. Roberts, 2019). What's more agonizing is predators being allowed back into classrooms afterward. Purposeful, intentional abuse of children happens regularly in schools. We must not be naïve. School personnel are human beings like everyone else. Like the rest of the world, they have underlying issues that go overlooked. Recent stories in the news prove some educators are determined to harm your child. It is not efficient for most, but some specifically look to work in low-income communities to get away with harming Black babies. Their infractions rarely lead to complete terminations. The need in some communities for teachers is so high that they end up back in the school system. Also, certain states have unions that make it impossible to terminate educators. I have been on the other side of disciplining staff for wrongdoing. There are cases where I compiled statements, text messages, pictures, and social media posts to detail a person's infractions. After fifty pages of records, the staff member was given a verbal warning and placed in the same school or another in the same district.

To protect our children, we must use specific tools to enable students to share their thoughts freely. By the age of four, your child should be able to name the majority of his or her body parts. Because many parents and teachers are uncomfortable discussing genitalia, preschoolers survey the body in this way: "This is my head, neck, arms, hands, chest, stomach, legs, and feet." What's missing? Your child should understand that the penis, vagina, and bottom are all parts of the body, just like their arm or leg (Family Education, 2021). When my firstborn went to school, there were critical words that my wife and I taught him. We made sure all of our children could articulate the proper names for the genitals and essential phrases. We familiarized them with phrases such as, "Do not touch me there," "That is inappropriate," "Do not verbally abuse me or behave sexually toward me," "I feel uncomfortable," and so forth. These are all alarms to possible abusers in their school. When predators realize that your child understands the complexities and meanings of such terms, they move away. Such language communicates that a child's parent is in their life.

Listen to Your Child's Body Language

There is a long list of physiological changes children go through. Sleep patterns, posture, speech, and many other aspects of their bodies change. As they develop physically, their personalities also shift. Pay attention to patterns when they arrive from home after school. A great way to understand your child's body language is by watching them interact with their teacher. At parent-teacher conferences, make sure your child speaks directly to the teacher. Notice if they avoid eye contact, speak with low confidence, or try too hard to appease the teacher. These are vital signs to consider. I train my children to talk directly to staff, with confidence, at all times.

Please speak with your child about their dreams. Most dream theories contend that the function of dreaming is to consolidate memories, process emotions, express hidden desires, and practice confronting potential dangers. Experts assert that children dream due to a combination of these reasons rather than any one particular theory (Cherry, 2021). If your child has nightmares about monsters yelling at them, this might indicate something is happening in the school that you may want to address. For Black children specifically, they are policed like no other race in schools. If they have nightmares of being restrained and locked away, it may result from being overdisciplined in school. Your child may be constantly restricted from being human. Just talking, smiling, and bathroom use are suspension-worthy infractions. Breathing too loud can land Black children in trouble. This abusive disciplinary environment changes your child's confidence and manifests itself in their subconscious. Their ability to walk with pride is compromised. I've seen confident Black children start to hang their heads low in the presence of specific teachers. As a father, I've had to argue with teachers about how they interact with my children. You'd think I didn't have to, being an administrator for over a decade. But I'm Black. My education and career mean nothing in the face of racially biased teachers. Educators take their students' actions as personal attacks. The worst thing you can do as a parent is notice such changes and blame your child. Responding like this to a child is shameful.

Staff members are not always right and can be quite deceitful. For example, a twenty-year veteran teacher from southern New Jersey, Karen Ledden, admittedly lied about her credentials. She presented false documents to the Board of Examiners during a job search because her husband was unemployed and her son's medication was expensive (Leibowitz, 2011). This information may be a shock, but teachers are flawed humans like everyone else. We as parents cannot overly discipline our children based on the account of any teacher. Consider how many parents must have spanked, punished, or verbally abused their children based on the advice of teachers. Race, gender, social class, and other factors impact how we view the behaviors of children.

Many Black families subconsciously want teachers to think they are strict parents. Therefore, when their children misbehave, we are quick to beat them without asking a single question. We all have biases, educators as well. Unfortunately, no one is fully aware of their prejudices. All races have been socialized to have a negative view of Black students. It is not wise to entrust your child to a single teacher's discernment. Take criticisms of your child with a grain of salt and never publicly shame or discipline your children.

Overdisciplining Black Children

The Black body has been vulnerable to racial domination through centuries of slavery, lynching, sexual violence, reproductive legislation, surveillance, segregation, mass incarceration, police practices, and popular culture. In response to systemic brutality, Black parents degrade their children through harsh physical punishment. Few parents, however, see spanking as abuse. Instead, most regard it as an essential component of Black identity, good parenting, and responsible citizenship. Black parents' devotion to spanking is rooted in genuine fear of Black suffering and arbitrary violence at the hands of white people (Patton, 2014). Parents overreact because they have a deep fear of what will happen to their children if they are not extremely strict with their children from the beginning. I have a friend whose mother believed in this way of parenting. She would regularly curse out and beat her children in front of me. Witnessing such abuse was confusing, as my mother rarely hit me. As time continued, my friend was referred to special education. Sadly, she did not graduate and developed a mental disorder. My friend's sibling became sexually active with older men. The violence that their mother passed on to them eventually happened among one another. They would get into fistfights and even used deadly weapons against one another. One friend was sent to a mental institution, and the other was living in fear of being killed when the other sibling was released. What is my point in sharing this? I believe that this level of aggression has long-lasting implications. There is nothing positive to be learned from abuse. Authentic transformation happens through honest dialogue. Teachers may see the abuse and choose to join in.

Early on, I made the mistake of being unnecessarily strict in front of my children's teachers. I was insecure, wanting the teacher's validation. I would give my children a stare or authoritarian tone for the teacher's entertainment. I believed it was best for children to know that education came first. Even before my love for them. How pathetic of me. In those instances, I wanted their teachers to know I was a stern Black father. What my children needed was what all Black children need in those instances: reassurance. They needed to know that we would hold them accountable but not destroy their trust in us as parents during the process. While public shaming is happening, children will try to connect with their parents and communicate an apologetic demeanor.

Praise your child publicly and discipline with wisdom privately. Beating or publicly disciplining any child is similar to buck breaking. The humiliation and shame have long-lasting negative implications psychologically. There is nothing more damaging than a parent publicly shaming their child. We are accustomed to believing abuse is justifiable. We say things like, "I had no other choice but to spank my child." Choices such as punishment, seeking outside guidance, or letting your emotions subside are all skipped over. Parents draw a self-serving conclusion that physical violence is the best elixir for parenting; it's not. Hitting children to "fix" any unwanted behavior stems from not having the social-emotional tools to effectively parent one's children. Such parenting is lazy and creates an unstable living environment for Black children.

Abusive Parents Are Worse Than Racist Teachers

Racist teachers have been here since the beginning of time. Hiding in plain sight in schools throughout America. Even with such persons in classrooms, Black children have been able to excel, in spite of such behavior. Honestly, it is a part of American culture. On the other hand, abusive parents confuse Black children. With one hand, the child receives love and, from the other, a closed fist. Black parents must consider where such parenting behaviors began.

Why do we do this? Why do we believe the best thing to do is beat, shame, and verbally abuse our children in front of their teachers? Deep seated within most Black people is a desire to impress white people. We are so desperate for them to see us as equals. When we are given positive reinforcement for our behaviors, no matter how violent, we feel better about ourselves. This belief stems from a history of Black people thinking that shaming one another will possibly gain respect from white people. If we are truthful, such strategies work. Blacks have received praise because of horrific acts done against their brethren. Fear pushes many parents to be rigid. We reason, "Let me beat my child up, so the world cannot." Our hostility is a demented expression of protective love. We don't want them to be hurt, so we overreact and hurt them so they can be powerful. Writing this seems weird, but this is how some Black parents think. My mother didn't physically discipline me too much. Once in a while, I can admit, I truly deserved it. Other parents would call her weak for not hitting my siblings and me. She reasoned that physical violence would last for a little. After a while, our bodies would grow accustomed. Instead, she softened our hearts, opened our minds, and used her influence to change our behavior. Many in the Black community consider having egalitarian conversations with children as a "white" thing. Parents, break the cycle. Physical discipline is rarely needed and only changes behavior temporarily. Abused children are in danger of becoming socially awkward, overly sensitive adults who resort to violence when conflicts arise. Violence creates long-lasting consequences that we cannot change later.

Your Child Will Tell On You

The behaviors and temperament of children first entering school are a direct result of their households. No matter how much parents try to hide what happens at home, the children usually tell on their parents about their behaviors. We (parents) try to play cleanup, and it is a bit too late. Children are confused, thinking, "Should I listen to my parents' actions or behavior?" Where I grew up, knowing how to defend myself was the center of every conversation. For my mother, a single mother raising three boys, it was imperative that we all knew how to fight. I would be told time and again that if someone hits me, I'D BETTER HIT THEM BACK. Not defending myself would lead to a world of trouble when I got home. Fighting was a pass to go outside. Turning the other cheek meant you had to stay home. Younger children have difficulty deciphering when another child is intentionally causing harm or simply playing around. As a result, they are unable to make critical decisions about self-defense. I dreaded the thought of going home to say I was a coward. No parent wants their child to hit or be hit by another child, but we do not realize what we are creating in our children at a young age when violence is the answer.

Walking away from a conflict is difficult to teach within the Black community. Unfortunately, some of us live in environments that don't permit the opportunity. Consider the foolish reasons we tell our children to fight. Parents have even gotten arrested for assaulting other children to "defend" their own (Barnhart, 2021). Others force their children to fight for absurdity. To my shame, I have come close to doing so as well. Once, my son was accidentally bumped on a playground; I almost caused him to fight a close friend. What was I thinking? Rarely are children deliberately seeking to harm other children. They are evolving, changing, moving, and developing quickly; expressing emotions is a new concept for them. By forcing your child to fight every person who bumps into them, you make your child seem disturbed. As a result, they develop antisocial behaviors that impact their adulthood.

Parents must consider that some teachers simply have poor classroom management skills. Even when children are in a structured, well-organized, instructional environment, fights take place. Teach your child to be critical of interactions, asking themselves several questions. "Has this person hit me before? Do I usually have a good time with this person? Are we friends? Do they share? Do they have issues with other people? Is the teacher always correcting the other person's behavior? Could it be me?" Training your child to think reflectively improves their thought process.

We are all socialized to have contradictory views on violence. For myself, violence was a rite of passage. When having children, we project internal values subconsciously. Our children have not and, God willing, will never have to fight as much as we did. Because of our hard work, they live in loving homes. Parents, be affectionate with your children, take them on trips, and visit the local religious institutions every once in a while. Allow them to live normal lives. Parents go through a mental time warp and prepare children as if they are living in the past. They are not in the *Warriors* movie trying to get back to Coney Island. They are not gang members preparing for a turf war. For parents, our realities and social norms are different from our children's. We were raised in a different time. Like Jay-Z said, "Hov did that so hopefully you won't have to go through that." Our struggles do not have to be our children's struggles. They do not have to earn war scars and make it out of the hood. That movie is played out. Walking away from a fight does not make anyone less of a human being unless this is a paradigm that you have developed within them. Sometimes it is okay to simply tell an adult that something is happening. When they start to take matters into their own hands, they end up worse as adults. Instead, teach wisdom, discretion, choosing friends wisely, and healthy communication skills. Doing all of this on your own is a lot for two parents, let alone a single parent. Thinking of the work can cause some of us to become disheartened. In the African tradition, we must go back to having an *Ubuntu* (I am because we are) mentality.

COMMUNITY MATTERS

The importance of a Black child's racial, ethnic, cultural group cannot be overstated. It molds their perspectives on the world and supports how they mediate mutual lived experiences in school. In addition, students tend to model what they experience with extended family members and the community (Tatum, 2017). Creating and participating in community groups is essential for Black families. In kindergarten, new parents and students are going through a world of transitions. Raising a family in isolation leads to increased errors. We have moved away from relying on the family as a community. A Westernized parenting style has negatively influenced our community. Futile competition with other parents have become more important than racial solidarity. Support groups guide topics that are unfamiliar to parents. No one's good at everything. What new parent knows every academic subject, every vaccine for children, the curriculum, school calendar, and so on? Some people do, but the average parent needs help. We live hectic lives. Parents get migraines just thinking about their child's school stuff. Use your village. Divide responsibilities, and come together. Share drop-off/pickup responsibilities, exchange contact info, have dinner together, and babysit each other's kids. Historically, we overcame through collaboration.

Each successful Black family has a support team. We must return to a community mindset. To do so takes humility. It is a prerequisite for joining any community of people. Participating in community signals, "I do not have all the answers." Develop trusting relationships with people who can provide mentoring. Many of us fear being this vulnerable, as this may make us seem unintelligent. Secretly, only thoughtless people try to independently fix problems that can only improve through a group effort. Parents fear dealing with a negative interaction with another parent we hold in high regard. Negative interaction is bound to happen; we are human.

We all have tried to be a positive community group when things haven't gone well. It could have been a church or a book club. Trying to make friends and play nice in the sandbox has led to someone betraying us. Traumatized from past hurts, we have become afraid to continue in new relationships. How do we move forward, entering new support communities with a history of negative interactions? How is that even smart? In life, we will have a host of support communities that will come and go. Friendships often serve a purpose for a particular time during a given season of our lives. Other times they are for a lifetime. We have to have realistic expectations of the life span of friendships. We say things like, "I need a community of people who are honest and real." "I can't stand being around fake people." Okay, if our prerequisite for being in a specific community is that everyone in that community is transparent about their thoughts at all times, we are being delusional. People are dishonest with themselves, fake, phony, and whatever term you'd like to throw in there. It's called the human condition. Included in this group of people are you and me. No one is truthful all the time. The person that we all lie to the most is ourself. Therefore, when we go to the parent-teacher conference meeting, we can quickly judge all sorts of people "fake," including ourselves. We are all flawed people with great intentions. We shouldn't befriend people based on biased proclivities. Let's focus on people who are caring, loving toward children. The underlying issue is that we turn down joining communities because we place ourselves above the needs of our children.

My wife asked me to join a parental training group in my son's elementary school. The trainer was from New York University, I believe. I felt uncomfortable when first attending the group. The trainer tried her hardest to engage the group by telling jokes and providing light snacks. Because I developed antisocial behaviors from childhood and negative experiences as an adult, I kept quiet. My wife pushed me to participate and speak a little more in the group. The more I participated, the more fun I had. Long story short, I had a great time. We learned a lot and built friendships with other parents along the way. I still wrestle with antisocial behaviors, but I have learned that it takes a village to raise Black children. We still practice some of the things learned in the group some twelve years ago. More core values about the ineffectiveness of physical discipline came from that course. As Black parents, we cannot miss out on such learning opportunities. We are not going to be best friends with everyone in our groups. Solidarity doesn't mean that we all think, act, and speak alike. It means that we have one similar goal, which is giving our children the best educational experience. Furthermore, do you want to only be around people who parent like you? That is an extreme level of arrogance. To believe that how we parent is the best way is a prison reserved for the unwise.

Historical Reasoning for Division

The origins of our divisions stem from what took place when we were stolen from our motherland. Conflicts among African American groups are directly caused by the prevailing white racial framework, in which vulnerable groups, incapable of fighting the forces that oppress them effectively, attack themselves or individuals who look like them (Okonofua, 2013). Precolonial African culture honored the community. Tribes shared similar language, customs, traditions, and the like. We developed systems of hunting, domesticating animals, making clothing, and mastering several languages. Much of our history has been erased due to Europeans' desire to stain our history. Slavers used Africans to enslave their brothers, sisters, mothers, and fathers. I doubt Africans who captured other Africans understood the extent of their actions. While enslaved, we started to communicate and consider ways of escaping. When slavers saw Africans speaking, this frightened them terribly. As a result, slavers began to find new and creative ways to isolate people from their community. These destructive tactics gave more power to slavers and less to enslaved people. Once in America, Black unity became a matter of life or death.

Black Communities on the Plantation

Slavers started to tear Black people apart as they first arrived on plantations. Black people's emotional connections were manipulated to keep control of their bodies. Blacks were not allowed to marry, be affectionate, or even smile too much. Such behavior was punishable through severe public beatings. Black mothers would beat their children and call them ugly to keep their slavers at bay. Slavers who caught wind of an intelligent young Black man used extreme tactics. Buck breaking destroyed Black men's confidence as shame clouded their desire for advancement. Beautiful young Black girls were used as sexual favors as well, creating separation between genders. This form of abuse caused Black folks to conceal all emotional ties to avoid any form of punishment. They got married in private, worshipped in secret, and became conditioned to not openly love each other. During this time in the Black communities on plantations, a new form of racial hierarchy developed. Colorism became an additional way that Blacks were divided and continues to cause tensions in our community.

Divided by Colorism

The boundaries of the Black community were formed by an informal "one-drop" rule, which, in its colloquial definition, provided that one drop of Black blood made a person Black (Hickman, 1997). The brown paper bag test was another example of discrimination based on skin color (Pilgrim, 2014). Intraracial tensions grew as lighter-skinned Blacks were favored by slavers, while darker-skinned Blacks were forced to work in cotton fields. Along with being able to work inside the homes of their masters was the constant threat of sexual assault. Our oppressors discontented with their sexuality, they turned to Blacks. Black women were repeatedly raped and gave birth to biracial children. These children were treated a little better than other enslaved people because of their skin tone. They were given opportunities to enter the big house and serve slavers. Darker-skinned Black folks were relegated to working in the fields. Because of this, Blacks started to have tensions with one another. Darker-skinned Blacks wanted the same experiences as lighter-toned brothers and sisters. Light-skin Blacks began believing that they were better than others. We lost so much of our sense of community and began mimicking the vile behaviors of our oppressors. Our facial features, tone of voice, and dress style became absorbed in Eurocentrism to avoid further harm. Colorism presently continues to divide our community. Some of us are so warped in our thinking that we do not even identify as Black. Some Latinos who initially came from Africa make every effort to avoid identifying their African roots. Regardless of how much we try to change, we must understand how socialization into a white supremacist country has divided our people.

Our Ancestors' Bones

Deep within the recesses of our spirit, we carry our ancestors' trauma, pain, and tensions. Slavery has destroyed the foundations of our culture so much that we believe hating one another is customary. I always have to correct my tone and attitude toward my brothers and sisters when there is a conflict. Our battle is not against one another. On a larger scale, it isn't even against other races. The struggle is against a system designed to remove the joy of learning from children. Whether we are aware or not, our children imitate our core values. They watch what we do more than listen to what we say. Telling your child to be an excellent Black scholar means parents must be examples of such standards. In our work, marriages, and communities, we must model excellence. Other races take cues from how we interact with one another. Displaying solidarity at all times speaks volumes.

Chapter 2

Middle School

The Middle Passage

When transported from Africa across the Atlantic, our ancestors were stored on ships as chattel. Their journey is now known as the middle passage. Africans were grouped in small confines and considered cargo; their humanity was stripped from the beginning. Contorted bodies lay in human excrement while women gave birth and nursed their young adjacent to rotting corpses. Medical attention wasn't needed for the "cargo." After leading tribes and ruling nations, royal families became freight. You could imagine the mental trauma that many experienced. They probably asked, "What wrong have I committed?"

Our Black children suffer similar traumas as they move throughout the educational system. Beautiful Black babies become predators in the eyes of racist adults as they move from elementary to middle school. Educators now treat them as adults with full awareness of their behaviors and actions. Teachers' microaggressions bias educational policies, and a bleached curriculum dulls students' imaginations. The shackles of state exam–based Westernized education holds students hostage. By the time they reach the middle passage or middle school, they struggle to comprehend the purpose of education.

GROWING BODIES

A significant growth spurt occurs throughout puberty, usually between eight and thirteen for girls and ten to fifteen for boys. Puberty lasts between two and five years. This growth spurt is linked to sexual development, which includes the appearance of pubic and underarm hair, the growth and development of sex organs, and the onset of menstruation in girls (Desiraju, 2021). As Black children's bodies mature, the world immediately engages them as adults. Our baby boys become taller, stronger; they start to look like young men. Society envisions our twelve-year-old boys as adults. In junior high, I recall the fearful stares I received. Rocking Method Man braids and listening to the Purple Tape didn't help. My mother allowed me to get the Big Daddy Kane parts in my eyebrows. My "predatorial" façade was a total contradiction of my personality.

As a preteen, I enjoyed drawing and writing short stories. Both mediums became outlets to relieve stress and communicate emotions. My aunt encouraged me to write stories and read them out loud. My imagination ran wild. Regardless of the plot, characters, or objective, she positively reinforced my passions. Once she took me to a local art store for supplies to channel my dreams. In my community, a love of artistic expression in junior high school would get you beat up. Few friends or family knew about my black graffiti books and short stories. In junior high school, you had to be tough, French-kiss girls, and wear name-brand clothes all at once. I tried to follow the hood codes. I fought a little, tongue-kissed a few girls, and stole my brother Mike's Polo gear. I was transformed into a new person. Presently, this transformation starts earlier with our children. Our babies' bodies are quickly changing, and they are unaware of what is occurring. They are exposed early on to sex and drugs and trained to be narcissistic from seven years old. I can't tell you how often I say, "Give your brains a break from electronics" to my children and students. As society changes and we grow older as parents, it is imperative that we critically analyze our perspectives.

PARENTING MATTERS

Wisdom, patience, and humility are required when parenting Black preteens. As Black parents, much of our discernment comes from lived experiences. We believe and force our truths onto children unwaveringly. Our ways of addressing children are according to our judgment and nothing else. Feedback, suggestions, and opinions from others are not relevant in our eyes. Children immediately disengage when we make these traditional, antiquated statements: "Well, when I was your age" and "Growing up, I would never . . . " My children usually take a deep breath and prepare their minds to think about everything besides my words. Recent events with COVID-19 and technological advances make generational comparisons invalid. There's not a parent living who experienced a pandemic as a child.

Insidious racism toward Blacks is our shared reality. Little has improved since the inception of racism as an American tradition. On a global scale, racism is more deadly than any human pandemic we have ever faced. With other outbreaks there are momentary pauses. We can receive vaccines, and take off our N95 masks to periodically breathe fresh air. Not so with racism.

There is no mask to block the scent of racism that is all consuming. Vaccines such as DEI (diversity, equity, and inclusion) programs have a low rate of long-term efficacy. Because of the unrelenting power of racism, parents must educate themselves on how to raise children in such a hostile environment. Researching best practices for parenting and teaching Black children is mandatory. Learning is a precondition for teaching. When teaching our children, it's imperative to qualify statements. Parents saying things like, "I may be wrong" and "This is just my perspective" gives children space to disagree respectfully. Children need to feel that dissenting will not end in physical violence. There is literature on parenting that we must read to ensure we're correctly raising our children. There are videos, websites, audiobooks, and support groups that make learning easier. If we don't take time to understand what's happening to their ever-changing bodies, we will continue inflicting needless trauma. Patience is a necessity when learning. I use the term "patience" because few of us have the time to think critically about our actions. We work exhausting jobs, deal with marital issues, experience health problems, and so forth. Considering better approaches to parenting feels like a luxury that many Black parents do not have.

Research indicates a strong difference in self-concept during middle school transition for Black students. Compared to elementary school students, middle school students show significantly lower academic performance. In addition, findings reveal that school transition to middle school is associated with a lower self-concept (Onetti et al., 2019). We go from holding their hands while walking to elementary school to throwing them a few dollars on the way out the door. Our children still need parents to be involved. We shouldn't transition children to middle school in an abrupt manner. Some preteens aren't mature enough to handle complete independence after being oversheltered, while others are overexposed. Both extremes negatively impact children when given authentic freedom. Black children also have to cope with the added pressure of their color. We must measure our students' preparedness for middle school based on their personalities. For example, if you have a child who's an introvert or has poor anger management, be cautious. Many of them still need affection, tenderness, and supervision for a bit longer. Being a late bloomer doesn't make them weak or soft; it makes them human beings. In pride, we project beliefs about where they should be according to our experience at their age.

Humble Parenting

Humility is a prerequisite for good parenting. My son Junior repeatedly mocks how I walk, talk, and behave. When I am upset, happy, or irritated, he knows. Junior loves exposing my dirt; it's his favorite pastime. He has taught me more about myself than any other person I know. Jennifer and I urge our children to argue with us if the evidence supports their claims. Junior, who is now fifteen, has developed a passion for law because of our rule. He loves getting into conflicts with us about our regulations and revealing our faults. As a parent, I must model humility when my children correct me. Being a lifelong learner is something all parents must embrace. Presently, our children are listening and learning at an accelerated pace. They observe, analyze, and make educated decisions on several topics. The traditional strategy of forcing compliance from children is ineffective and only creates insecurity. In humility, parents must realize that we no longer have all the answers because our lives would be a little different if we did. We are talking to middle schoolers about academic excellence, peer selection, avoiding gangs, all the while never addressing our bad choices. Parents portray a false picture of perfection and will eventually damage bonds with our children to maintain this gilded persona. Parents lie and kids know it. Adult men tell young men to respect women, yet our relationships with our wives are toxic. Older women tell young ladies to be independent without explaining the importance of developing healthy boundaries. Parents justify lying using mantras such as, "They are too young," "We have to protect them," and "Don't ruin their innocence." All self-serving paradigms that protect our egos. The older our children become, the more self-reflection becomes a necessity.

Parents have trouble humbling themselves to children. We deem meekness as weakness and apologizing to children as absurd. Many parents believe in scolding "disrespectful" children. If this is our rationale, what should happen to a parent who models low standards, drops out of school, has a turbulent marriage, or gets divorced? What is that parent's punishment? We hold children to higher standards than ourselves. Abusive, self-righteous parenting may work momentarily, but eventually, Black children develop negative behaviors as a result. To be clear, disciplining your children is crucial to their growth. But we must do so humbly, knowing that we fall short on several occasions. Acknowledging faults does not make us weak parents. Instead, it demonstrates trustworthiness to our children. Our consistent, long-lasting dependability is vital to our children's middle school experience. As their bodies and minds mature, parents must also mature in their ability to demonstrate compassion.

Parenting the Mind

Black children entering middle school go through a wide range of psychological transitions that will shape their lives. I was clueless when I started middle school, creating imaginary worlds that did not exist. Peer pressure and a toxic sense of masculinity clouded my judgment. Also, in my community, it was understood that "nerds" got beat up after school. To avoid such a fate, I took on the role of court jester to stay out of harm's way. Joking was a form of self-defense in my neighborhood. If you could crack jokes, rank, or partake in the *dozens*, people tended to leave you alone. Whether through self-deprecation, or insulting someone else, Black children use this as an alternative to fighting. For myself, I loved laughing at myself and others.

The burdensome reality of racism was an additional barrier I would have to face. The staff was a bit more aggressive and harsh toward the Black boys. One teacher seemed to love antagonizing Black boys by ripping our hats off and yelling in our faces. Most teachers were kind and understanding and did their best to engage learners. But it was always this one teacher who appeared not to have sat at the "cool" table when younger. They used titles to abuse authority and get revenge for their younger selves. Such teachers must address unconscious biases before entering schools. Implicit bias training should take place prior to hiring new staff members. Universities should have an extensive course listing for teachers entering the field. Presently, there are one or two courses focusing on culturally relevant DEI pedagogy. There are few experts in the field who have lived experiences and a well of research in the field. Moving forward, teacher certification should include additional courses geared toward such sensitive topics. Additionally, after teachers are hired, there needs to be ongoing training. Bias resurfaces, ebbs, and flows. Similar to a seasonal flu shot, we all need ongoing professional development. Being conditioned in an American society that has normalized bias requires intentionality to avoid the spread of the virus.

Practical Application of How to Attend to the Psychological Needs of Preteens

High parental expectations have been linked to high academic attainment in studies. Setting unrealistic expectations, on the other hand, is detrimental, according to a recent study (Anderson, 2015). Parents who set unrealistic academic expectations for their children risk jeopardizing their children's mental, emotional, and physical well-being (Kendrick, 2021). We want them to comprehend topics we've never explicitly taught. Additionally, variance among cultural norms isn't a priority. Educators from backgrounds dissimilar to students' are unaware of their lived experiences. Differing cultural understandings and students' life cycle development further complicates standard expectations for diverse students. Black children develop differently than other races because they face problems that different ethnicities do not. For example, Blacks learn to hate themselves at very early ages. The doll experiment performed by the psychologists Drs. Kenneth Clark and Mamie Clark exposed how Black children are socialized to view themselves as "bad" starting as early as six years old. Their self-perception is forever negatively impacted because of how society views them. As students, they are viewed as problematic, troublesome, and in need of alternative educational settings. Positive and negative reinforcement based on race impact their development in school and beyond. Teachers must take that into account when educating Black children.

Our students reside in a society that has not historically favored Black youth. Stating that Black lives matter is now seen as a political ploy. From Emmett Till to George Floyd, Blacks religiously are slain without accountability. Media dulls our senses to inhumane brutality against Black people. Black children are intentionally traumatized then told having an education will fix all their problems. My son Jonathan, who is now thirteen, feels fatigued for no reason. When I ask why, he states, "I am just tired of having to deal with racism." The freedom to naïvely think the world is full of kindness no longer exists. He's aware of society's obsession with destroying his being. As a parent, I do not have the luxury of not having intense conversations about race with my babies.

Traumatized by racism, middle schoolers have trouble processing layers of emotion. Other races do not have to shoulder such burdens. As early as five years old, Black children have to deal with adult issues. They have to navigate schools that have teachers who have been trained to hate Black people from birth. As a consequence, their childlike innocence is permanently scarred with every death caught on video. Such psychologically paralyzing trauma causes many students to burn out. Why would they want to continue being in the presence of such negative energy? Constantly being suspended for minor infractions, being referred to special education for minor reasons, and dealing with microaggressions from teachers. Brilliant Black minds never get the chance to fully flourish at their highest potential. They become survivalists trying to make it out of school alive. Then, once the damage is done, and the student no longer desires to be in school, fingers are pointed at the Black community. The educational system blames victims while never taking a glance in the proverbial mirror.

Conversations between adults (both educators and parents) require transparency and impartiality. Discretion is necessary when addressing topics such as academics, race, sex, hormones, and puberty. Traditional methods of discussing these areas are ineffective. Adults have unhealthy, self-serving communication practices. Many adults assume, "Well, if I figured it out on my own, then I guess my students/children should as well." Another toxic form of miscommunication is boldly misinforming students on topics we learned the wrong way. Some of us were taught bad habits by broken people, while others use social media as parental guides. Both extremes are unhealthy for our children and careless. A majority of adults have not learned to have a healthy, equitable dialogue with children. Generational differences stunt our social-emotional intelligence as Black parents. In certain instances, we have to converse with other parents. Asking for help isn't a weakness. It is the highest form of intelligence that society appears to diminish. Friends have strongly advised me to be sensitive when scolding my children; I thank God they did. They cared for me enough to stop me from fracturing my relationship with my children. Back parents are all experiencing similar difficulties, but we are too proud to admit it. Refusal to seek assistance leads to children learning from media, society, and their friends.

TRIBAL AFFILIATION

Black children begin going through a tribal affiliation in middle school. I usually can observe it best in the cafeteria. A tribe refers to one's social division in society, one's family, peers, and community, connected through economics, culture, or blood ties. In Black communities, peer groups have a significant influence on children. The implications of choosing specific peer groups can positively or negative impact a student's performance. Most students make decisions about peer groups based on their desire to fit in according to perceived identity formation. Forming one's identity has to do with how humans establish a unique view of self. Thug, rapper, basketball player, or football star: these are the prevalent stereotypes that most Black children mimic. Those who chose to be scholars are picked on the most.

Bullying isn't a simple interaction between aggressor and victim. Peer groups/networks support and sometimes participate in this behavior (Laninga-Wijnen et al., 2019). Students fight for popularity by associating with specific groups. Social capital is used to gain visibility and admiration. There are labels for each group. You have the popular table, baby gangsters, nerds, jocks, and so on. Most kids assemble according to elementary school relationships. Slowly, social hierarchy forms while eating lunch, and unintentionally, parental guidance fades. I remember sitting in the lunchroom with people from my housing projects. I've known these guys my entire life. We'd travel to school daily and hang out afterward. Joking around was like a second language for us. I had to grow thick skin because everyone received the same treatment. Eventually, I accepted the rules of snapping, cracking, jokes, and the dozens. Unfortunately, some guys were out of my league. The best jokesters sat at the popular table. I saw an opening to sit with them, and I took it to my shame. That mistake led to me being joked on. My beat-up Reebok shoes, crooked line-up, and tight Bugle Boy khakis didn't help. At that moment, I realized my tribal affiliation was with a different set of friends.

Peer group selection is critical, especially for Black children. Relationships in middle school have enduring implications.

As parents, we must explain this phase of school thoroughly to our children. Some of us use blanket statements like, "Stay to yourself," "Don't let them bother you," "Tell the teacher," or "Punch them in the face if they bother you." Out of fear, mixed with love, we provide unrealistic solutions. We have to assist them in understanding how to analyze personalities, and selecting the appropriate tribe. I have long conversations with my children and their friends to ensure they are aligned. A quick statement to parents: if we are still trying to sit at the cool table, our children consider us frauds. I've met several adults who haven't accepted adulthood. Living through children by purchasing designer clothes sends a confusing message. Middle school peer selection is complicated. Regardless of their decision, be familiar with your child's peers at all times.

Parents who speak negatively about their children's friends can push a massive wedge into their relationships. Our children hold their friends in high regard. They become easily influenced by their peers' every utterance. My mother was transparent and balanced about her perception of my peers. She'd give precise descriptions of each person. She religiously acquainted me with the consequences of following specific individuals. She'd say, "You will end up dead or in jail following that guy." I knew she was right and that her words came from love. Also, when she misjudged a person, she apologized. Our words and advice as parents remain with our children for a lifetime. Regardless of my mother's warnings, I rebelled. In my mind, she didn't understand what I was up against in middle school, and I didn't have the time to explain. She made walking away from peer pressure seem so easy. I believed that no matter how I tried to explain my perspective, she just wouldn't understand.

Sayings like, "Well, why don't you just" or "When I was your age" immediately provoke children to become defensive. Comparing ourselves to children benefits no one. Every generation faces diverse challenges—all generations of Black folks hurt in distinct ways. We've never had it easy. Comparative oppression is still oppression. When your middle schoolers have issues, seek to find common ground and parent accordingly. Storytelling is a huge component of the Black tradition. African literature was destroyed when Blacks were enslaved. To ensure that our history continued, stories were passed from generation to generation. The oral tradition continues and is a valuable tool to teach our children. As an educator, I personally use stories that positively impact my students' behavior. Stories of failure, conflict, academic success, anger, hurt, and frustration are shared to relate to students. I also use such stories for professional development when training teachers. It takes a great deal of vulnerability, but I have found this practice to be more effective than anything else. Parents should consider passing on stories that illustrate their points without having a heavy hand. Tell of instances where you faced obstacles and persevered. Counternarratives give children resources of experiential knowledge without forcing obedience.

Adolescent rebellion is necessary for preteens and teenagers to grow. They are fighting for independence and control, struggling for peer acceptance, and experiencing extreme hormonal changes (Brennan, 2021). Black parents are personally offended to give children guidance and have it ignored. When our child asks for further clarification, we scold him or her for asking questions. My mother had moments when questions weren't allowed, but she articulated her reasoning most times. She wouldn't just say, "Shawn, I want you to stop hanging with that person." She would ask questions about the person: "Who do they live with?" "Do you think they would tell you to do the right thing?" "If you robbed a bank, do you think they would tell on you?" Or she would refer to something they said or did and ask me how I felt about it: "You know he curses at his mother. Is that cool with you?" "You know he drinks, that okay with you?" I knew what she was alluding to, but I didn't feel forced to take her advice. I followed her advice because it made logical sense.

The possible consequences of my actions have been instilled in me from birth. I had a father who was in prison. He was an ever-present reminder of what happens when you choose to break the law. Having that prompt stopped me from being around the wrong crowd on several occasions. Even from prison, my father always shot straight with me about his decisions. He'd say, "Keep it up, you'll be here with me, and they don't take it easy on little boys like you." Mom would say, "I have no bail money or a car to visit." I had no delusions of grandeur or expectations that she would help me out in a jam. "Grown man actions come with grown man consequences," she'd say. I still had that rebellious façade, but I never crossed the line. My façade protected me from looking "soft" or "weak." Imitating the tough guys in my hood, I pretended to be indifferent. On occasion, I'd raise my voice just a little to see if I could intimidate her. It never worked. She would simply remind me of the option of leaving her home, if I felt inclined to do so.

Too many times, parents aren't aware of the importance of being honest with their children. When children know the truth yet their parents contradict it, the children begin to distrust themselves (K. Roberts, 2014). Dishonest caretakers cause children to become insecure. We are shielding them from reality in a way that will hinder their growth. No one is always going to be there to clean up their children's mess. Why create a false reality? Adults saving the day at the last minute does not develop Black children's character. Some of our children are under the impression that their actions have no penalty. Such unrealistic thinking harms children. Early guidance around delaying gratification and possible consequences teaches self-discipline. The earlier our children embrace structure, the better their adult lives will be.

One day, my friends and I spray-painted all over Starrett City in East New York. We tagged our names with red Krylon paint. Being a follower and wanting so desperately to fit in, I went against my better judgment and hopped a train from Rockaway to the Pennsylvania Avenue station. We walked out of the train, shook up the can, and began tagging everything in sight. Every plexiglass bus stop, storefront, and apartment building had our names. Filled with adrenaline, we felt invisible. We weren't. We got back on the B6, going down Flatlands Avenue to catch the B60 toward Brownsville. A pair of detectives stopped the bus and made us get off. My heart left my chest and rested in my throat. Without an escape route, we were handcuffed and placed in the back of a Ford Taurus. Weirdly enough, after initially getting caught, I wasn't afraid.

The three of us came from a crime-ridden community. Getting arrested was a badge of honor. Boastworthy bragging rights were granted to people who did time. Denying all allegations was our strategy. Our plan had promise until my friend stretched out his arms. In cinematic, slow motion, a red can fell out of his army jacket lining. In unison, we burst out laughing at one another. All of our parents were immediately called. My mom and aunt were the only guardians available to pick us up. When my mother entered the precinct, the fear of God seized me. She was never one for embarrassing me in public, which was worse for me. Her death stare was impeccable. While signing papers for my release, her gaze was on me. More than a beating, I feared disappointing my mom. She had poured so much into me. I never wanted her to feel unappreciated.

The Importance of Reasonable Consequences

A large part of child development is understanding how consequences work. However, logical consequences vary from natural consequences in that they necessitate the intervention of an adult—or, in the case of a family or a class meeting, other children. Therefore, it is critical to determine what type of consequence will result in a beneficial learning experience that will inspire youngsters to choose responsible collaboration (Nelsen, 1985). The consequences of me spray-painting led to me being punished and staying away from certain friends. However, those same childhood consequences produced academic responsibility, an emotionally intelligent husband, and the ability to raise three exceptional children. Lessons such as respecting authority figures and choosing peer groups wisely have positively impacted all aspects of my life. Failure to teach these lessons early leads to more complex dilemmas in the future.

Understand What You Are Going Through

To my little Black brother and sisters in middle school, you hide your intellect well. Adults try to force-feed you information you already understand. Wanting to fit in and be popular is expected at this stage. Adults become forgetful of their experiences and hypocritically lecture you way too much. We have good intentions and poor delivery. We don't want an unwise choice to alter the direction of your life adversely. As preteens, know that your actions carry consequences. Society has no remorse or forgiveness for you. You don't have to listen to everything your parents preach, but reflect on the important stuff. Begin envisioning the life you want and ask, "Is my parents' advice in alignment with my goals?"

BLACK MIDDLE SCHOOL TEACHERS

In recent years, there has been a greater drive to recruit more teachers of color into the classroom, frequently revealing huge disparities between student and teacher demographics.

According to national data, the issue is not just hiring but also keeping those instructors (Barnum, 2018). Black middle school teachers face unique hurdles as professionals. They work in hard-to-staff schools in low-income communities. As with most schools, Blacks are a minority of the school's instructional staff. Of an already small percentage, Black men represent less than 2 percent (Whitfield, 2019). We carry the responsibility of speaking on behalf of the entire Black race. These problems represent the burden and consequences of tokenization. We are involuntary guides on diversity, inclusion, equity, race, and gender. We must call our students to excellence while being considerate of the environments they traverse. Confronting the microaggressions of false allies is an additional burden. Administrators tend to devalue our intellect but call on us to police lunchrooms, hallway transitions, and school dismissal. There is no wonder the turnover rates for Black educators are so high.

I have several colleagues who speak with me about what it means to be a Black middle school teacher. One is a special education teacher who has been at her school for over a decade. She is extremely cautious when bringing up racial issues with colleagues. We spoke once about how staff members react to diversity training. When training happens, several teachers roll their eyes and text one another in disgust. The best tactic by the cynical staff is deafening silence. She takes note of comments about students labeled as troublemakers, hostile, and destructive. All if not most of the students are Black. Her conservative, passive demeanor allows her to listen to the utter disgust her colleagues have for students. She informs Black students of how they are perceived. In return, students express their disinterest. When speaking with their parents, she is too "rigid." She lives in an educational chasm. Her voice is ostracized by colleagues, overlooked by students, and lamented by parents.

What Should Black Middle School Teachers Do?

Black middle school teachers must not allow themselves to be typecast into traditional Joe Clark characters. Joe Clark, a high school administrator in Paterson, New Jersey, established a name by brandishing a bullhorn and a baseball bat (Hyman, 1989). Morgan Freeman's portrayal is the role Black teachers are expected to maintain in schools. Classroom management is an issue at all school grade levels, especially in middle school. It is not our job to keep order in the entire building. Assuming roles as police officers to calm unruly students should not be mandatory for Black staff members. Disciplinary leadership roles are freely given to Black teachers because few others want the position. Administrators expect us to break up fights, confront angry parents, and save the entire community. Irrational expectations lead to further burnout and turnover. To ascend the school hierarchy, you may temporarily take disciplinary positions but always display your intellectual prowess. Sadly, we must compromise to develop social capital in educational settings. Also, our children respond more positively when we intervene. Our compassion mixed with an innate understanding of Black culture gives us an advantage. Unfortunately, some of us get too comfortable in such roles without developing other skills. Diversifying one's skill set is vital in any profession. Facilitate affinity groups, support colleagues, provide solutions to the administrative team, and speak up during professional development. By doing this, you make your long-term intentions clear. You communicate, "I am tough, but more importantly, I am intelligent and able to lead in several capacities."

What Should Ambitious Black Teachers Expect?

Ambitious Black educators must prepare for backlash from the school community. They will face small, passive forms of racism throughout their career. Microaggressions may appear insignificant when experienced once or twice, but they take a toll on a teacher's psychological well-being over the course of years, if not a lifetime (Terada, 2021). Stepping up as a leader in any school comes with consequences. You will be alienated, laughed at, and treated adversely by those you once called friends. You will have to cancel all emotional ties to people who give you negative energy. Constant discouragement will eventually make you resign. Subconsciously people want you to know your place. Your dreams illuminate others' shortcomings. When colleagues try to suppress my dreams, I now feel pity. How pathetic is their life that they seek to mock someone's aspirations? Always remember your purpose. You are there to provide hope for Black children, not to make friends.

The Wrong Friends

During the 8th grade, I folded under peer pressure. I officially joined a neighborhood gang, went spray-painting, shoplifted, and got into a few fights. I was looking for friends in all the wrong places. Eventually, I found a gang that took me in. My name was changed, and I went through an initiation. Deep down, I was terrified, knowing that violence and death came with the territory. Fistfights were something I could deal with, but the crew I ran with took things to a new level. Stabbings, shooting, and extended jail time were on the menu. I sank to the bottom as the waters of peer pressure washed over me.

Our children are facing intense peer pressure that is nearly impossible for them to handle on their own. There is a perfect storm of emotions, hormones, insecurity, and socialization taking place simultaneously. The façade of social media makes adolescence psychologically torturous. Before the invention of cell phones, fights were seen by no more than ten people. Everyone else gossiped about what happened. Presently, one scuffle can be seen internationally by millions. Could you imagine getting beat up in front of the entire world? Kids' embarrassment from these incidents has led to depression, anxiety, and in some cases, suicide. Students do not want to become a meme. They risk the danger of becoming a permanent satirical image. Unable to cope, young people turn to opioids and increasing gang violence. Archaic parental advice like, "Walk away" or "Just keep to yourself" doesn't work in some circumstances. We have to provide realistic solutions. Children shut down, realizing they are speaking to a person who has no clue of the world they live in. Preteens become silent and act as if they are obeying your rules while planning to do the opposite. To help our children, we must realize that their existence could never compare to our reality as children.

A FATHER'S ROLE

As a preteen, I realized that I was entirely out of my mind. I knew that I wasn't making the wisest decisions, but I could not care less. My dad was locked up, and my mom had several responsibilities. I was able to get away with more than others because she had three boys and couldn't see everything. Even though she was busy, she did one thing that altered the rest of my life. She reached out to my dad. He was informed of my name change, hanging out all night, and following crowds. My dad had been in prison for approximately ten years when I was in middle school. He spent most of his time in maximum security state prisons. He kept friendships with lifers and had a few brawls with corrections officers, landing him in solitary confinement. He was my definition of *tough*. When I told him of my gang involvement, I thought he'd be proud. He was not. He felt ashamed that he had raised such a coward, and he let me know it.

The phone call I had with my dad about my gang activity changed my life. Up until this point, I'd had pleasant conversations with him. He would send me paintings, wood carvings, and belts he'd made while working in shops in prison. He also would scrape together a few dollars and send me checks for $20. These $20 checks were a small amount of money to my naked eye until he reminded me that his hourly rate was seven cents—a little more than seven weeks of work at forty hours of work a week. I understood the value of money because of his small gesture. On a phone call to Rikers Island, I proudly told him my new name and gang affiliation. He sat silently, providing little feedback. When he spoke, his tone was different. I could hear him trying to hide rage. The most dangerous feeling is when he would pause and take a deep breath to gather his emotions. He explained how personally offended he was about my actions. Each question he asked exposed, without explicitly saying so, my cowardly heart. "So you joined because you needed friends?" "You were trying to fit in?" "So now you are telling me not to call you Shawn?" he asked. He stated, "I want to hear you say that to me directly. Tell me not to call you, my son, Shawn." My body stiffened. I was sure that my harsh, killer, gangster dad would be proud that I was following in his footsteps. I couldn't have been more wrong.

From what I knew about my dad, he was a no-nonsense guy. He let his actions do most of his talking. Every time I asked him about his criminal past, his silence said more than his words. I asked him questions like, "Did you ever rob someone?" "You ever shoot someone?" He would just remain silent. He never confirmed or denied any of my questions. I guess he was trying to protect me in a sense. Because of him, I know they're lying when I hear "gangsters" publicly discuss their criminal activity. His obvious displeasure with my gang involvement possibly saved my life. His assertiveness is what I needed. He ended the conversation by saying, "You are a coward for joining that group, and I am ashamed of you." At that moment, my stomach dropped. Holding back tears, I told him goodbye and hung up the phone. I never realized how much I needed my dad's discipline, validation, and approval until that point. Black parents sometimes step back when their children are in middle school. At that moment, my dad stepped in, and I believe that experience saved my life. My mother's greatest strength as a parent was knowing when her impact ended and working collaboratively with my dad would succeed.

Realizing that my dad's words came from a pure space, I made it my mission to drop the gang as soon as possible. The following day, I avoided attending a weekly gang meeting. Intentionally, I went to play ball with friends. Unexpectedly, the gang member walked past my apartment building when I was walking home. Approximately twenty gang members started calling my name and asking me to speak. Every part of my body wanted to run. Realizing that I would have to run for the rest of my life if this continued, I faced the group. I could feel my father's words pounding on my conscience: "You are a coward," "I am ashamed of you." Finally, the leader asked, "Why didn't you attend the meeting?" I replied, "I had to get my little brother." That was the best lie I could conjure at the moment. They began circling me, and I knew what would happen next. The punches came from every direction. Someone pulled my jacket over my head. Trying to impress my dad, who was one hundred miles away, I fought back. I lost, but I fought as hard as I could. An older gentleman came to my rescue and broke up the fight. In pain but full of pride, I went home. I was out. Taking my beating like a "man," I could now face my father. I wrote a letter informing him of my exit. He was proud. My hero leaped from behind iron bars and guided me during this crucial part of my life.

Black parents, we must lean in more as our children get older and rely on one another. Evidence shows that resident and non-resident Black fathers positively impact both the psychological well-being of single mothers and their child's behavior (Jackson, 1999). We are overly confident in their ability to handle what they are facing. Most parents want to be involved in their children's lives, but the pressures of life interfere. Friction between parents negatively confuses children and forces them to pick a parent. I implore parents to set aside differences and be more attentive as the children get older. I've made the mistake of thinking my children needed me less as they matured. What I learned is that each child has different needs based on their personality, not their age. Preteens are not full adults ready to handle the burdens of this world. Children living in single-parent homes could use the support of their father. Just a few words of encouragement could change their lives. My mother told me everything that my father said, but she is not my father. I needed to be admonished by my dad.

Single Mothers and Absentee Fathers

Single mothers too often carry the entire weight of the family. That statement is simply the truth and not meant to point fingers. Maternal burnout syndrome affects single parents, particularly Black women. In addition, some individuals obtain depression and anxiety symptoms due to balancing the full responsibility of parenting (Lebert-Charron et al., 2018). Along with single mothers, the emotional trauma children develop is disastrous, and the repercussions last for several generations. What makes this experience even more painful is how Black mothers and fathers interact while children are present.

Throughout my childhood, my mother never spoke ill of my father. I knew something had gone wrong between them, but my mother held her biases to herself. She'd say, "You will learn all about your father when he gets out of prison." Her restraint afforded a path for me to connect with him on my terms. Unfortunately, many mothers treat children, especially their middle school Black boys, with disdain because of issues with their father. Regularly seeing the father's likeness in their child causes many Black mothers to transfer negative emotions to their boys. These young men are unaware of their infraction or the cause of their mother's wrath. As a result, the hostility children experience transfers to peers, siblings, classmates, and other relatives.

When mothers speak negatively about their children's fathers, they develop everlasting contempt. My mother did the opposite. She'd say, "Your father and I had a horrible separation, but that doesn't mean he was a bad father." She didn't allow her trauma to become my own. There are some fathers whom Black mothers need to keep far away from their children. Some fathers are irresponsible and abusive, and protecting a child from their presence is the best thing a mother can do. But some fathers would love to help out. They may not have the best jobs or the most suitable backgrounds, but they have distinct expertise to save their child's life. I say this as a warning not to place unnecessary stress on our children. They should not be used as bait or placed in the middle of arguments.

Involving children in disputes is one of the most abusive things parents can do. As words fire across the room, the little ones become casualties. Children become insecure with no parental assistance from both parties. I've heard parents use incendiary language toward one another in front of children—conflicts at home transfer between parents, children, classmates, and teachers. Schools then rush to label Black children as needing special education services. Children are then held responsible more than their parents. The mental abuse of hearing parents berate one another conditions children to become abusers. Parents should praise one another publicly and respectfully correct one another privately.

Professional support is required at times for undealt-with internal trauma and conflicts with others. Systemic treatments, such as family therapy and other family-centered methods, have a favorable influence on children's behavior (Carr, 2014). Therapy provides an environment to discuss conflicts in a healthy manner and learn new parenting strategies. Parents have triggers from their past; if ignored, they ruin relationships between spouses. We then project internal problems to innocent Black children. Parents who separate should make it clear with their children. Reassure them that parental separation is not their fault. Reinforce this message regularly. As a kid, I secretly believe my parents' separation was because of me. I become obsessed with fixing it. Preteens start thinking deeply about the world, race, sexuality, peers, and other relationships. They question society and want to make an impact. I had the strangest thoughts about what was happening with my parents. I thought, "Probably, me being born was the issue." I just knew that if I weren't around, they'd be back to normal. As I grew older, I realized my parents' separation was their decision. Whether I was born on not, they more than likely would have separated anyhow. What gives me this confidence? For one, both parents assured me that their issues had nothing to do with my existence. Additionally, the percentage of Black couples that divorce is approximately 75 percent. Children being born is not the number one factor. There is freedom in a child knowing that their existence isn't the cause of so much sadness.

Fathers, Be Honest

According to research, those who had a good relationship with their fathers as children are less influenced by stressful events than those who had poor father-child ties (Novotney, 2010). Part of a "good" relationship is transparency. Fathers, be honest about who you are, early and often. Eventually, your children will find out anyway. What I love about my dad is his honesty. His truth gives me the ability to have a clear perspective. When I asked him about what happened with my mother and him, he made it plain. "Things didn't work out, and I was outside doing my thing," he said. "I was in the streets trying to make fast money and dealing with different women," he said. His integrity erased my insecurity. Too many times, fathers lie and confuse children about separation. Fathers say things like, "Yeah, things didn't work out, your mother didn't change, I was unhappy." These statements tend to leave young Black children confused. Which parent should they trust? There is no ownership on the parent's part, leaving the child to blame themselves. The best thing a father can do is be honest. As the saying goes, "Speak the truth and shame the devil." Here's an easy one-liner: "I wasn't the man I needed to be for you and your mother; I am sorry." Without providing clear answers, you leave children to find role models in the wrong places. As they go in negative paths to fill emotional voids, their behaviors seem rude to educators. Teachers wrestle with a sense of entitlement and narcissism and cannot see that children have issues at home that hinder learning.

GOOD VERSUS BAD TEACHERS

Educators, sometimes intentionally, create an extra layer of trauma for students. During the 1980s, JHS 275 was notoriously dangerous. There was an awkward teacher who loved to provoke students for no reason. Let's call him Mr. G. Mr. G was white, approximately twenty-five to thirty years of age. He had a mullet buzz cut, a thick mustache, and he sweated profusely. He felt it necessary to be the school disciplinarian, though no one asked him. He found pleasure in chasing kids in hallways, taking off baseball caps, and cracking corny jokes. Everyone thought he was a little weird, but no one paid him any attention. We were too busy being kids, I guess. One day there was a fight on the third floor. Mr. G jumped into action to save the day. His form of breaking up a fight was a bit on the aggressive side. I could envision him watching the show *Cops* while practicing restraining techniques. He was quick to shove people and put students in wrestling choke holds. The faculty ignored him because they refused to get involved.

As two boys were fighting, Mr. G went into Hulk Hogan mode. Out of frustration, one boy pushed Mr. G, and a fight ensued between the teacher and the student. Cops came in, and the student was led out in cuffs. I didn't see the student again for the year. He would wait for friends at 3 p.m., but we rarely saw him in class. Unfortunately, teachers often cause more harm than good. Instead of sharpening his choke hold skills, Mr. G needed professional development for social-emotional intelligence, restorative justice, and conflict resolution. Our children need more than teachers well trained in multiple restraining tactics.

Many teachers have a superhero mindset while working in Black school communities. In particular, many white female teachers embody the bountiful savior archetype. The self-perceived role is to save underprivileged, at-risk students from the plight of their communities. Films such as *Dangerous Minds* and *Freedom Writers* illustrate the archetype in urban classrooms of Black and Brown youth (Mackin, 2014). They believe their God-given mission is to save Black kids. In low-income minority communities, you find an assortment of educators who are teaching our children. Some of the most dedicated, hardworking teachers are in these schools. Also, there are staff members who couldn't find employment anywhere else. The latter group outwardly seems concerned about transforming lives, but their motives are self-centered. They survive in these environments because few people want to teach under challenging circumstances. They spend more time thinking of ways to discipline children and less time developing healthy relationships with families and students.

Identifying Good Teachers

In each school, there is always one teacher who has the respect of the community. In the schools I've worked in, there are teachers with the power to silence entire auditoriums with a glance. I have vivid memories as a student of teachers like Ms. Yovanna, Ms. Grimes, and Mr. Williams. They wouldn't allow me to slack for a minute. I could have been a fantastic student, but I did just enough to stay off their radar. I understood the work, but I had no drive. There were no immediate benefits in view. Ms. Yovanna was repulsed by mediocrity. She was petite and had Brown skin, and her handwriting looked like calligraphy. She reminded me of Phylicia Rashad, beautiful, intelligent, and strong. Learning was a matter of life or death in her eyes. She was well organized and structured, leaving little space for a court jester like myself to get away with anything. In middle school, we spent most of our time in homeroom class, and then we had a few electives like gym and art. Regardless of what trouble we gave other teachers, she would have none of it. God forbid she received a bad report from her colleagues. Recess would be canceled; extra homework and phone calls to parents followed. Her eyes closed the entire classroom's mouth. Parent engagement was her most significant leverage. Threatening to call parents was backed up by swift action, with pure intention. Though we hated her discipline, we respected her tremendously. Sometimes not being disciplined makes you feel unloved and neglected.

Our current political and racial climate makes the teaching profession unattractive and confusing. Some teachers are too strict without having a genuine relationship with students. Others believe students earn sensitivity after they pass an exam. Performance-based kindness is conditional and eventually fades. Slavers aren't considered nice based on perceived kindness toward high-performing enslaved Blacks. Conditional, performance-based kindness hardens the hearts of students. They become numb to our requests. A gentle word to children is more influential than any disciplinary action. These children are facing poverty, crime, and hunger; living in single-parent homes; and so forth. Your school suspension threats aren't effective.

Many teachers try to relive their childhood by being "cool." Students aren't held accountable for their actions and suffer academically. A deficit model clouds their judgment. Teachers justify thinking, "Well, look at where they live. Give them a break." Subtle, hidden racism of low standards is the most destructive. Subconsciously, Black children regularly hear that they are incapable of greatness. Coddling students without healthy boundaries doesn't help them become scholars. An enemy multiplies kisses, but wounds from a friend can be trusted. The educational system has been compromised by capitalism and politics. Educators are terrified of providing feedback on student's academic performance for fear of seeming racist or insensitive to the struggles of Black students. The result is that Black students are not receiving quality instruction. We should be sensitive to such issues and simultaneously speak honestly with students. Social promotion, lowering standards, and passing students for optics harm children. Educators become enemies of students by way of passivism. As educators, we have to prepare students for the real world. How does an educator avoid being too harsh or too soft? How do we find balance?

The first step is taking ownership of our influence over student behaviors and outcomes. Schools are sites of inequity that encourage underachievement among African American students; as a result, instructors operate as agents of the system who build and sustain a dominating culture through activities that are incompatible with the academic output of young Black children (Kenyatta, 2012). Accountability of classroom management and disciplinary skills begins with educators. I remember being told by a veteran teacher that discipline represents 75 percent of a teacher's job. The percentages fluctuate based on race and wealth. Students of all colors understand the importance of rules and regulations. They crave structure. An educator's core belief about quality education is recognized by how they discipline students. Most teachers make their motives and intentions clear. They are not working in the classroom to get rich. The lessons they teach transcend school settings and prepare students for life. The majority of teachers rarely attempt to punish children. Consequences of inappropriate behavior are reasonable and expected from the student. Ultimately, they want to get students back to learning. Bipolar, emotion-based teachers seldom get the best out of their students. Students silently lose respect for abusive teachers and rebel to avoid further interactions. Colleagues privately identify incapable staff. Conflict averse, many teachers do not like holding one another accountable. When teachers cordially correct one another, teachers with healthy disciplinary practices avoid egotistic thinking.

Fearful Teachers

Fear-driven teachers do everything in their power to avoid disputes. Parents, administrators, colleagues, and students paralyze them from standing for anything. Living lives void of any conflict and then transitioning into working in an urban setting is a disaster waiting to happen. Students realize they can easily manipulate staff members. In the long run, students suffer academically because underneath their teachers' masks of coolness lies unceasing fear. The story of the emperor's new clothes comes to mind. Teachers are the audience members who are too afraid of informing the emperor of his folly. Students represent the emperor improperly dressed, laughed at, and mocked. All the while, fearful teachers gain notoriety as the "relatable" teacher with the new

Jordans, quoting Drake verses. All along, students suffer. These teachers love sharing action stories with friends and family. I say this not to discourage teachers but to help them change how they see their roles in the lives of Black children.

Our Hood Hero, Mr. Will

The savior of our middle school was a safety agent named Mr. Will. He was approximately five feet seven inches tall and built like a tank—a man of meaningful actions and few words. Junior High School 275 housed several children from neighboring housing projects. Within a five-block radius, the school is next to several dangerous government-subsidized housing complexes. Van Dyke, Tilden, Noble Drew, Marcus Garvey, and my housing projects Riverdale Houses are within walking distance of one another in Brownsville, Brooklyn. So we took on the identity of where we lived. The violence occurred as a result of conflicts between rival housing projects. I rarely understood the beginning of disputes, but I was obliged to join in. If a person didn't help when fighting, they could no longer go outside. If one person from Riverdale Houses was fighting someone from Tilden, it became WrestleMania. Before many of these battles began, Mr. Will intervened.

He had a great relationship with all the students. He would give us high fives and talk to us like an uncle. Honestly, he had more power than the principal. We respected his words more than our teachers.' He was from the community. You would see him in the barbershop or shopping for groceries in the Key Food on Rockaway Avenue on a Saturday. In the middle of the most dangerous neighborhood in New York City, he was comfortable. He knew the drug dealers, gang leaders, and pastors. But, when it came to discipline, he was harder on us than any other staff member.

His methods were unorthodox but understood in our community. My first experience with him in the 6th grade was interesting. While walking late to class, I heard Mr. Will yell out, "One, two, three, it's hammer time." Everyone cleared the halls immediately. I didn't know what happened. I asked a friend, "What am I supposed to do? Is this a drill?" He said, "If you get caught by Mr. Will in the halls after he calls out hammer time, he'll beat you up." "Beat up by who?" I said. He replied, "Play if you want to; I'm going to class." In my mind, I thought, "He can't do that. Isn't it illegal to get hit by a staff member?" I didn't say it out loud, though. There was a heavy price to pay in the street for snitching, especially on Mr. Will. The rule was you take your hits and keep your mouth shut. Now, let me place this disclaimer out there before your imagination runs wild. Staff members can never physically assault children. Mr. Will never harmed any of us. He would just act as if he was going to. The most he would do is tap us on the back of the head. He was always playing around. It felt good having a father figure who kept you in check just a little bit.

Value Experiential Intelligence

There are people within the neighborhood who may not have an educator's title but have substantial power in the school community. Mr. Will was one of those people. Teachers must learn lessons from these individuals and seek their guidance. They have experiential wisdom that will propel your practice to an entirely different level. Often these individuals solve problems after they have already taken place. Instead, seek their insight in a preventive manner. The cafeteria lady, janitor, security guard, and school aide have relationships with students that we can use to guide our practice. If we do not value support staff based on their job descriptions, our students miss out on their hidden gifts and natural talents.

THE IMPORTANCE OF PHYSICAL ACTIVITIES

Middle school students form a large portion of their identity through sports. My mother made me play every sport available. Sports became a way to deal with frustration, tension, and stress; express emotions; and develop lifelong friendships. I began a lifelong friendship at eleven years old with someone I now consider family. Boxing was the sport that brought us together. We grew up in the same housing project, Riverdale Towers. When he first moved to Brownsville, he was a soft-spoken, quiet kid. He wasn't born in Brookdale and shipped right to the projects like everyone else. Being the new guy led to him getting teased and bullied. His light-skin complexion and Spanish language made it worse. After experiencing the trauma that comes with bullying, he started to fight back. His heart grew callous from fighting daily. He had the power of a heavyweight, which was strange for a kid weighing 120 pounds. What made matters worse for opponents was his ability to take hits. Regardless of his street accolades, he was still just a silly kid in my eyes. He never wanted to fight; the environment gave him no choice. In his home and on the street, defending himself was a necessity. We became best friends in the most uncomfortable fashion.

My cousin and I were walking back home from middle school. My cousin was my age and desperately tried to fit in. He was flashy and boastful and drowned himself in Brut 33 cologne. He lived in a private house on Strauss Street, away from the projects in Brownsville. When he'd come around, people left him alone out of respect for me. We had fun, but he had annoying habits. He would try to hang out with people from different projects, and switching sides wasn't allowed in Brownsville. He spent time hanging out in rival housing projects. One could never tell if he was a friend or foe. I am not sure exactly what took place, but I can remember when my cousin and my best friend were about to fight. My best friend (we'll call him Tim) and my cousin (I'll call him John) were arguing, and I went to see what was happening. Now, I wasn't going to fight Tim because he was my friend and I wasn't going to fight John because he was my cousin. John decided to threaten Tim. John said, "I am going to stab you." At that moment, I knew things were going to go wrong. You see, Tim would rather die than allow someone to threaten him and get away. Tim grabbed John's hand with the knife and placed it on his neck. Tim pleaded, "Please stab me, please, I beg you, please stab me in my neck." Like, I said, he would prefer death than allowing someone to intimidate him. Ultimately, I intervened, and both of them went their separate ways. Since that time, Tim has been one of my closest friends. After that incident, I checked in on Tim to see how he was doing. He explained the reason he could not allow anyone to harm him physically. At that moment, I didn't feel fear or threatened by his intensity, only sorrow. I realized the origin of his core pain. He then told me that he wanted to go boxing with this older guy from the neighborhood.

Fighting Is Good

Boxing was never my thing, but Tim eventually convinced me to try it out. I learned how to defend myself a little bit from my brother. Being able to protect yourself was mandatory in Brownsville. I had no intentions of ducking bullets and getting into street combat daily. I tried to be tough, but it never really fit me. I am a joker by nature. Tim was also, but the streets forced him to become something else. I saw his heart harden as the years passed. Fortunately for us, an older gentleman from the neighborhood started taking kids to the boxing gym. Tim was looking for a way to channel his anger and avoid street fights. Boxing was the perfect outlet. Before the beginning of the 7th grade, we began training. Our trainer, Andre, picked us up for roadwork around eleven in the morning. Everyone in the neighborhood would mock us, saying, "Y'all can't fight." "Why y'all trying to be like Tyson?" Running was excruciating. Tim was in good shape, and I was affectionately known as Mike's chubby little brother. Each morning we ran for approximately two hours. Later, we would rest, wait for our trainer to return from work, and walk three miles to Starrett City Boxing Gym. The journey to the gym was the most dangerous part of the day.

Most of our childhood memories took place traveling to the boxing gym. The trip required walking through five different housing projects. Each day felt like an episode of *Survivor*. There were so many rules and codes in my neighborhood one must know simply to go to the store. Various projects had beef, and knowing this information could save your life. Tim and I understood the redlining throughout Brownsville. East New York was a different world. We would walk, sneak on a bus, or take a train without a train pass during summers. Each day it was a new adventure. We were chased and nearly jumped on several occasions. But, with our newfound boxing skills, we didn't mind. After being chased and trying to maneuver violent environments, we trained for three hours at the gym. The gym felt like home. A broken-down basement, smelling of sweat, musk, and mold, we were in heaven. The smell was bad, but purposeful. Having a reason to stay off the street and out of trouble was essential to my survival. As students, we had to balance being athletes and getting good grades. More importantly than the sport itself, we stayed out of so much trouble happening in the neighborhood. We would come back and hear about close friends who were murdered.

Black students desperately need physical activity. Team sports are more than just a form of exercise. Sports have a profound impact on the lives of young people. Physical exercise and intellectual achievement are inextricably linked. For example, a University of Kansas study of high school students discovered that more than 97 percent of student-athletes graduated, which is 10 percent higher than students who do not participate in sports. Athletes' GPAs were likewise shown to be higher than nonathletes (Malsen, 2015). Besides the physical benefits, they need fellowship, friendship, and structure. Parents should start their kids out early and often. Not all Black children have to play basketball, either. There are free soccer, lacrosse, tennis, and track-and-field teams they can join. Obesity, depression, and anxiety rates for our children are skyrocketing; they've become lifeless beings. We cannot allow them to lock themselves in their rooms for hours on end. There are life skills that only sports can teach. Without consistent physical activity, students enter schools filled with tension.

Teens Read Energy Well

Black students can read people from a mile away. Educators—and parents—cannot hide who they are. Black students can differentiate between authenticity and perpetrators. They have a heightened sense of assessing someone's character. Being able to do so is a form of self-preservation. Teachers must speak truthfully. You will not be able to mislead them with hollow threats and promises. When you sincerely care for students, they know. Conversely, when you do not care, they also know. Black children know when/if their parents dislike them.

During preteen years, children transition away from being afraid of parents. Physical threats are null and void. This generation requires transparent, equitable conversations. They know when we exaggerate to get the point across. Overdramatizing issues causes them to lose trust in us as parents subconsciously. Empty threats and poor follow-through communicate hypocrisy. Stories of our childhood failures aren't aligned to the standards we project. Realistic expectations and transparency about our expectations build trust.

Chapter 3

High School

9TH GRADE

The high school experience is notably different for Black children. They have to contend with almost insurmountable suffering. They must deal with the plight of their skin while existing in a world intentionally designed for their demise. Some students develop low self-esteem realizing their best efforts will never receive the same treatment as other ethnic groups. Also, they deal with being ostracized from their community for trying to "act white," which is a term coined following school integration to describe the false relationship between academic achievement and whiteness (McWhorter, 2019). Even when trying to raise their expectations, their living environment creates a sense of fear for displaying their genius. The consequences for Black scholars are emotionally draining. Sadly, many students succumb to stress and surrender. Students, families, educators, and leaders must learn how to support Black students. Before college, they require extensive training.

Student Perceptions, How Teens See the World

I've had the opportunity to work with a wide range of Black students. The majority live in low-income communities and single-parent homes. Yet what always amazes me is how they can excel regardless of their circumstance. They've overcome many problems: teen pregnancy, homelessness, learning disabilities, learning a new language, and so on. Yet, with all of those issues, they surpass everyone's expectations, time and again. There are so many stories of success that continue to inspire my work.

I can recall a young man from the Dominican Republic who exemplified courage, strength, and assertiveness. He came to our school in the 10th grade. New to the country, he had to learn English. He regularly came to school in uniform, never got into trouble, and took his academics seriously. Often, students who primarily speak Spanish tend to spend time with one another. Linguistically isolated communities allow them to avoid speaking English publicly; this was not his case. He regularly communicated with English-speaking students, sat with them at lunch, and participated in extracurricular activities. He had no problem asking how specific phrases were supposed to be stated. He was comfortable laughing at himself when his accent slipped out. Students like him have a magnificent strength that propels them forward no matter the circumstance. He eventually took additional classes and advanced courses, and he passed his state exams to graduate on time. What he, like many others, understood was the power of having high self-driven expectations.

When students have high expectations of themselves, they become unstoppable. Research asserts that racial self-esteem and academic self-efficacy positively impact the educational outcomes of Black students (Saunders et al., 2004). Forcing students to have high expectations doesn't work. Fear is a short-lived emotion that changes over time. Conversely, expectations stem from a sense of responsibility to oneself. Students must learn to develop an intrinsic understanding of responsibility. When speaking with this specific student, others could see that his drive was straightforward—he had no one else to take care of him.

Students from low-income neighborhoods have an educational advantage that they might not fully realize. Students from regions such as Africa and Asia, including India, are more sensitive about the consequences of failing in school. They have a deeper understanding of how academic achievement correlates to financial stability. With little economic assistance from relatives, students develop academic grit like few others. Following street codes or complaining about homework isn't of interest. Obstacles in their path become stepping-stones. They are proud of their unmatched work ethic. The Dominican student I mentioned earlier contended with gangs and poverty. Yet he resolved to be successful. His steadfast resolve was apparent to the staff. His story is but one of many that happen all over the world. People in third world countries with no parents and few resources become doctors, lawyers, and scientists.

We sometimes look at cases of successful people from challenging neighborhoods as an anomaly. Their seemingly accidental achievements make others from similar backgrounds lose hope. Society makes Black excellence seem to be for a chosen few—a gift only bestowed on the talented tenth, W. E. B. Du Bois's concept, which emphasizes the importance of higher education in developing leadership capacity among the "most able" 10 percent of Black Americans. The rest of the Black community is regulated as the "mass" in need of leadership, according to the concept (Gates & Root, 2013).

The talents and exceptionality of Black people surpass 10 percent. Believing only a few were talented led to slavers poking and prodding Black folks who displayed their abilities. People wanted to know what made these Negroes so special. There was nothing special at all. When given opportunity and resources, Black folks are just as exceptional as any other race. In all arenas, sports, entertainment, science, and technology, we have dominated. Our impact is so powerful that patents for our inventions, our scientific genius, heck, even our culture is repackaged, Europeanized, and sold as a new trend. Presently, Black creators' content is being stolen and used by other races to make a profit. There is no difference in educational spaces.

In school, Black children undergo the same scrutiny. First, they experience alienation from insecure peers, afraid of seeming inferior. Second, different racial groups mock Blacks for their intellect. Third, even their teachers question the validity of their academic excellence. Education becomes an unresolvable dilemma or a cruel practical joke. There's no safe space to feel a sense of scholarly comfort. This steady isolation persists through college and into careers. As a veteran educational leader, I still encounter alienation. Many students drop out after realizing nothing they accomplish will give them the same respect as their racial counterparts.

Observing 9th Graders, Views from the Field

As an administrator, I have seen the academic enthusiasm of many students die in the first year of high school. Yet 9th grade is the most critical year of school for our children. The best place to observe student behavior is not the classroom but in common areas. Social learning occurs in the cafeteria, gymnasium, hallways, and walking home after school. In these areas, students' social interactions significantly influence their educational outcomes.

In the cafeteria, there are a multitude of social negotiations that take place simultaneously. I remember seeing a kid come into my school. He came from a good home and wanted to do well. However, his father had experienced a difficult life and desired that his son avoid such experiences. His mother worked in the Department of Education as a school assistant. She had also experienced trauma. They didn't live close to school. The student traveled about forty-five minutes to an hour each morning. He was quiet and respected all school rules. This behavior lasted the first two or three months; then, I noticed him chilling with a different crowd in the cafeteria. Some were gang related; others in the group just weren't about anything positive. As soon as he sat at the table close to the cafeteria's exit, I knew something was wrong. Guidance counselors and deans spoke with him, but eventually, he made his decision to join the gang. I called the parents up to have a conversation about what was happening with their son. The son eventually admitted to trying to fit in and being afraid. The father, who stood approximately six feet three inches tall and weighed 230 pounds, started to weep while hugging his son. He cried because he didn't want his son to turn out like him. He had recently come from doing time behind the wall. Realizing that their son wasn't built for street life, the parents eventually took him out and enrolled him in a district closer to home. Parents, few children can handle the peer pressure that comes in high school. Please pay close attention to their changes in behavior. For me, the cafeteria has become a lens into my students' world.

There is a stigma associated with particular groups in high school. Here are a few general descriptions to consider. First, there is the "nerdy" group. They play video games and talk about anime. Next, there is the "rock and roll" group. They are from an urban environment, but they do not subscribe to the urban profile like most students. They are okay with being called weird, corny, and the like. I enjoy the rock and rollers because their bravery pays off when they transition to college. Next are the "tough" guys. These students are usually the weakest out of the groups. They come into high school with a certain level of clout based on what they did in middle school. They are loud, obnoxious, and desperate to get attention by any means necessary. At this table, they play, fight, and curse each other. This group has the highest social capital in the cafeteria. The "tough guy/girl" table is where everyone wants to sit. Reading this as an adult, you may laugh, but the human condition persists throughout our lives. Many adults are still vying for a seat at the cool table. Humans want to belong. It looks a bit more sophisticated as we age, but the concept remains.

Before your student enters high school, teach them about social hierarchy. A society's classification of its people into groups based on socioeconomic factors such as wealth, income, race, education, ethnicity, gender, occupation, social status, or derived power is referred to as social hierarchy or stratification. The groups labeled "popular," "jocks," "floaters," and "good-ats" are at the top of the social hierarchy. In the middle, there are the "fine arts" kids, who have grown in popularity in comparison to previous studies, as well as the "brains," "normals," and "druggie/stoners." "Emo/goths," a new group of anime/manga fans, and "loners" are at the bottom of the social hierarchy. Depending on the participants' backgrounds, the positioning of "race-ethnicity" groups vary (Crabbe et al., 2019). Most students are unaware they are a part of the pecking order as they begin school. Please, be transparent about their status in the school's social order. My children are clear. They come from a loving home, with educated parents who make decent money. Acting tough would never work for any of my kids. There is no reason for them to mimic someone's else trauma to seem "gangster." I don't minimize their problems, but I also do not allow them to exaggerate their issues to seem relatable.

I learned my lessons from my father. He taught me about the dangers of sitting at the wrong table in prison. Doing so could end your life. He trained me to keep my back to the wall and my eyes open at all times. Watching people's behavior and keeping a firm demeanor was a necessity. Most of my lessons happened during jail visits. While speaking in visiting rooms, he would model how I should behave. Some of his lessons were a bit too intense for a teenager, but I understood the more profound lesson he was teaching—safety comes from wisdom.

For 9th graders, the same principles apply. They should sit by themselves or stand alone in the cafeteria. Doing so communicates, "I am not interested in joining a group." Standing alone takes strength and courage. They become a mystery to everyone by being reserved. If invited to sit at a table, advise your child not to. Why? First, they aren't familiar with what people do outside of school. Second, gangs are looking to recruit naive first-year students, and their motives are impure. Third, alphas usually flex their power by having large groups surround their table. Next, there may be a conflict brewing that is unbeknownst to your child. Ignorance will not be an acceptable excuse on the streets. Finally, when it's time to walk home, your student gets jumped and doesn't know why. Therefore, the smartest thing to do is sit alone for a couple of weeks. Sitting by themselves will provide the time to assess the crowd. After thoroughly evaluating the group, with help from their parents, they can make sound decisions.

Eating Free Lunch

Statistics indicate that approximately 72 percent of New York City public school children received free or reduced-price school lunches (NYS Student Report, 2021). Though most students qualify, publicly eating free school lunch is a big decision. Parent income polarizes most school districts. Most parents in the same geographically located schools have similar incomes. From my experience, students in low-income environments like to seem wealthy. Students believe in starving themselves rather than eat free school lunches. As a 9th grader on food stamps, Section 8, and Medicaid, I tried my best not to eat "free-free." That performance lasted a week. I encourage students to eat school lunch if they are hungry, but there is a practical strategy. Students, please, for the love of God, do not scarf down the food as if it is your last meal. You will experience ridicule for the rest of your life. You have to be nonchalant. Eat it, but act as if you don't need to eat. Do not be the first person on the line. I have seen students run to the lunch line with all their strength, sweating and choking while eating food. One student would pack his belongings early in class to have a head start. As much as we tell 9th graders, "What people say doesn't matter," it does to them. No one wants to be on *WorldStar* and be known as the "free-free" monster.

While on the line, chill out. Don't play fight and push one another. Instead, talk about something that has nothing to do with the school lunch. For example, discuss sports, boys, girls, or music, or play games on your phone. Then, respectfully grab your tray and make your way to your seat.

Gymnasium

In high school, the 9th-grade gymnasium is where reputations are built and destroyed. Most physical education classes have a few sports happening simultaneously. There are always students loitering on the sidelines, unprepared to participate. Sports provide students the chance to exercise during the day. Participation in high school sports is crucial to their experience. Sports participation differs between both genders. From my experience, most girls don't participate in sports because of their hair, sweating too much, or messing up their outfits. A former student intentionally decided not to graduate on time to avoid gym class. Like the cafeteria, the gym class has a pecking order, and students should understand the social hierarchy. First, there are the "jocks." These are students who play a particular sport, which leads to advanced physical ability and social capital. They tend to be the most popular students. Boys gain more popularity than girls because of traditional, biased gender roles, but this varies depending on the school. In larger sport-centered schools, girls are just as, if not more, popular than boy athletes. "Jocks" practice three hours a day, compete at a high level, apply for sports scholarships, and use sports as a conduit out of their community. Having students participate in sports automatically gives them a community, discipline, and structure that lasts a lifetime. Next, some students occasionally play for fun. They subconsciously know they're not that great, and sports is a social activity. Here is where I landed when I was in school. When boxing, I practiced with friends who became professional champions. I played ball with friends who later became professionals and Division I superstars. Sports was just a time for me to get out of the house. Then there are students who are uninterested in sports altogether but do what they need to do to get their grades. They follow the rules and do what is required to graduate on time. Then some students do not try at all. They come to school day in and day out and never prepare for gym class.

Solutions for the Gym

Students need to develop an appreciation for some physical activity when they are young. The beauty of physical activity is the variety. In most urban areas, kids play basketball, but many kids do not have the raw talent or work ethic to be a professional. Sports like lacrosse, tennis, and fencing can help Black students receive scholarships. We as parents and educators need to think creatively about changing the narrative that all Black children must play football or basketball. If there isn't a sport they are into, they can learn to train as a profession. A couple of years ago, a staff member started a weight lifting program. He would gather all the out-of-shape students who didn't have many friends and had them lift every day. Nutrition and a healthy diet were a part of the program. Day in and day out, you could hear the iron dropping to the ground on the third-floor multiple-purpose room accompanied by loud grunts and laughter. Presently, those students who have transformed their lives are professional physical trainers and police officers. More than transforming their bodies, they changed their minds. They became more confident in themselves through weight training and built a community of friends. A very small percentage of high school students play in college, and even a smaller number participate professionally. Participation in sports is not about selling false hope of becoming pro athletes. Sports unifies diverse students, and provides a safe space for expression.

Students must master something more than homework assignments and state exams. We train students to learn specific content areas that can have a lasting impact on their lives. I propose that high schoolers receive training in professional trades, which will provide immediate results and positive reinforcement. Having a deep understanding of global studies doesn't lead to direct financial compensation. Courses in financial literacy and entrepreneurship help students develop business models that can be utilized now. Also, social media has become a way for young influencers to earn a living while being students. Through sports, they learn life skills that supersede the classroom and develop soft skills that help in their postsecondary lives.

I played basketball and enjoyed boxing as a kid. I had no intentions of entering the next draft or being the next boxing champion out of Brownsville. But I needed something to keep me busy as a youngster. I didn't score the most points or even enter some games, but I sure enjoyed doing something positive with my time.

There was one time in particular that comes to mind. I would regularly go outside and just practice. Honestly, I just worked on flashy street moves. And one mixtape with Skip to My Lou was popular at the time. The public school across the street (PS 41K) was packed with competition. Late night in the park, there were always crackheads, drug dealers, and couples doing what couples do. The basketball court, for some reason, was left alone. I would go there until it got dark. One night, while shooting midrange shots, hot metal flew across the court. My streets smarts kicked in. I did what all hood kids would do. I got low. Being that shootouts happened twice a week, I wasn't nervous. At some point, I believed gun violence would be the reason for my death. Emotionally, I was numb. When I asked what happened, a friend said, "Sam was shot at close range in the head." Sam was in my elementary school. I'd known him my entire life. Survivor's guilt was heavy that day. Daydreams of me being Sam clouded my thoughts. What if I didn't have a sport that kept me occupied? Allow my survivor's guilt to be a siren to you, the reader. Parents and students, find a sport for occupying your time in high school.

In the four hours between 3 p.m. and 7 p.m., nearly one-fifth (18 percent) of juvenile violent crimes occur. As a result, the rate of adolescent violence after school is more than five times that of the juvenile curfew period, inclusive of both school and nonschool days (Juvenile Violent Crime, 2021). Parents have to pay close attention to their children's actions during those four hours. Idle time is poisonous for teens. Parents are at home or work, distracted by the tasks of being adults. Students are in a vulnerable position trying to figure out who to follow, stay away from, and so forth. A simple solution is to place them in sports that will keep them occupied and distracted.

Hallways

There is a science and art to functioning in a typical high school hallway. During transitions between classes, hallways are where most of the drama takes place. First, some students walk with a large crowd out of insecurity. Other students, uninterested in the nonsense, walk with one or two friends to get to class. Next, there is the person always running late or going to the bathroom in each class. They are more interested in everyone else's business instead of minding their own. Then, some students rush to class and refuse to let anything distract them. Walking the hallways teaches you a lot about the students' character that most parents do not notice. Parents should talk with their students about whom they sit with at lunch and whom they walk with to school. Educators also need to pay attention to their behaviors around different groups of peers.

The Desperate Mixer

When in high school, walking with large crowds through the hallways is the best feeling. You are letting people know that you have a crew and backup if a conflict arises. You get to show off your cool sneakers and clothes and crack jokes with your buddies. Periodically it is good to walk with your friends, but it often gets to the point where you look lame. You get desperate and start waiting for other people to tell you when and where to walk. Some students, if adults in the halls stop them from cutting class or making noise, choose to get loud, curse, and so forth. Remember this: the loudest one in the room is the softest. Many times, the students who are in these larger crowds are the weakest of them all. My dad said older men serving longer sentences would scout the youngest, loudest inmate to bully. Does this mean that you should not walk with your friends every once in a while? No. But also know when it is time to reduce the amount of attention you are bringing to yourself.

I don't want to sound preachy or hypocritical. I, too, was a desperate mixer in the 9th grade. I usually traveled with the kids from my housing projects in junior high school out of fear of being robbed. That fear traveled with me into high school. I went to school in the city (Manhattan). The Brooklyn kids stuck together to avoid having problems with the Bronx, Queens, and Manhattan kids. I followed suit because I was too weak to "be a man and stand on my own two feet," as my father would say. As a result, I traveled with approximately thirty guys daily. No one dared to bother us, and more people wanted to join our group. It wasn't a gang in the traditional sense, but we held one another down. Mobbing the halls and train station, we always got into some trouble. Walking toward the train station, we overflowed the sidewalks. At the moment, it felt like heaven, but there were future consequences to those actions.

Presently, as an educator, I realize a lot of friends were avoiding more profound learning difficulties. Not to sound arrogant, but school was never difficult for me, as it was for most kids in the group. Then, I started to notice that some friends were never in class. When they did attend class, it was for the gym or an art elective. I realize now that some were struggling academically and misbehaving to mask fundamental literacy delays. They'd say things like, "Oh, it's so tiresome," to disguise an attention deficit disorder. Others who always wanted to fight had several emotional disturbances. I deliberately transitioned to a smaller circle of friends who were more aligned with my goals. Black parents, train your children to understand these behaviors from an academic perspective. Just calling their friends stupid or crazy doesn't work. Use the correct terms, and help your child to decipher specific behaviors. Black teachers, use your stories to help our students. Some of us have gone through these experiences and forget. Use your struggles to be a guide for others.

CHOOSE FRIENDS WISELY

Students, there comes a time when you have to choose friends with a little more wisdom. When transitioning from a large group to a small group, you do not have to be weird. Measure your time wisely, and be balanced. There is a time and place for every friendship. Walk the halls with two or three friends; that's a good number. You may miss the popularity of being with a large group, but you also draw less negative attention. Build friendships with people who will have your back in the streets and push you in the classroom. Search for peers who have integrity are honest and have healthy social skills. Changing peer groups takes great sensitivity. Mishandling the change can undermine your high school career.

Parents and educators say things like, "Just stay away from this group" or "Only speak to this friend." Having students of selected isolated peer groups is dangerous. If they are getting jumped after school, their friends from AP English can write paragraphs in their defense. Conversely, their childhood friend who struggles with basic addition isn't going to help your student prepare for the algebra state exam. Different groups have social/intellectual capital that is of value to students.

Walking Away from Gangs

When I was a student, stepping away from a large group was challenging. The first time I did so was in junior high school. I associated myself with a group of guys who usually beat people up when they asked to leave. After having that fateful conversation with my dad, I informed the leader of my resignation from the gang. The conversation did not go well. Eventually, I knew the gang members were going to catch me slipping. While walking home from playing basketball at the local recreational center, I saw the gang from a distance. While I was trying my best not to be seen, they called my name. Now at this moment, running was not an option. If I did, I would have to run for my entire life. I faced the music. While being circled by ten gang members, one chose to blow weed smoke in my face. I am no thug, but I couldn't accept being disrespected in such a manner. Eventually, I swung, he swung, and the rest was history. The rest of his cronies started taking cheap shots when my jacket went over my head. My fear subsided, and adrenaline took over. I thank God and my dad for giving me the strength to face my anxieties that day. As a 9th grader, I found myself preparing to break away from my peer group again, but I wanted it to be different this time around.

I started distancing myself, being less available, and making up excuses not to be around. "Nah, son, I gotta go to class," "Nah, son, I gotta play ball," or "Chill, son, next time, I promise." "No, y'all don't have to wait up on me, I am good," I would say. I didn't want anything to do with the constant buffoonery anymore. Buffoonery that I was the ring leader of in the past. Humility was a prerequisite for distancing myself. What I didn't do was treat my friends as if I had no love for them. Although I still dapped them up and checked in regularly, I kept my distance. Eventually, people got the message and realized that I was about my business.

Lifelong Brothers

After leaving my large group in high school, I developed a lifelong friendship with two people I consider my brothers. Both of them were from Brownsville, Brooklyn, but were never followers. In humility, I began asking for their support and silently imitating their behaviors. They walked the halls, played around once in a while, but never allowed themselves to get too distracted. I followed their example. I was amazed at their ability to be friends with all groups and avoid extremes. They became the people I turned to when I needed guidance, and they still are.

Walking Alone

Some students aren't able to make friends. For whatever reasons, they are outcasts in school, never able to find their tribe. They walk alone and dance to their own tune. By choice, many isolate themselves from others, while others try to make friends but fail. Our young people's social skills have diminished tremendously since the invention of cell phones. They've become too engrossed in TikTok and Instagram to have a casual conversation. Virtual reality games and pranks consume their lives and further isolate them from building lifelong childhood memories.

The reasons teenagers choose to be in groups, remain isolated, or have a few select friends vary. Some students have been burned before by friends and do not want to be in compromising positions ever again. I've seen students betrayed by childhood friends and embarrassed over secrets they shared with friends. Because of that embarrassment, they choose to stay by themselves to avoid further conflict. Also, there are alpha males/females that are confident enough to stand alone. Most times, crowds follow alphas because the energy they radiate attracts others. Regardless of the cause, walking alone is ultimately a sign of strength few students possess. I chose walking alone and received a beatdown as a result.

Family dynamics will eventually shape how young people perceive themselves/others and the world. They will also have an impact on their relationships/behaviors as well as their future well-being. When every member of the family argues with each other in harmful ways, wounds fester. The causes are due to a poor parental style (abusive, authoritarian). Prolonged conflict can harm a child's neurochemistry, causing stress/insecurity and attachment loss (Ba, 2016). In turn, children begin having conflicts with staff members and students when in school

Parents, be careful about training your children to imitate negative social skills. Some of us grew up fighting everyone over the littlest thing. Getting bumped while walking or learning someone is gossiping about us meant we had to fight. We transfer these beliefs to our children and ruin their futures. They develop overly aggressive tendencies that isolate them from others. Other parents have been so isolated as children that we believe it is the best way to raise our children. We must train our children to be balanced and not fully imitate our behaviors. Ignorantly, some of us believe we made excellent decisions when in high school. We didn't. Many Black parents have lower back tattoos, triple-extra-large T-shirts, and fake jewelry, indicating we also made a few bad decisions.

In the 9th grade, there were rules and regulations to walking alone that I did not understand. One day I was walking to school. I traveled from Brownsville, Brooklyn, to Fiftieth Street in Manhattan. My school had a street between Eighth and Ninth Avenue that everyone used to enter the building. While walking to the building, I noticed a group of older students standing in two rows. As students walked through the two rows, the older students would trip students walking to school. Watching what was happening, a few thoughts came to mind. I thought, "If I walk across the street, I will look like a herb." I also thought, "I can run through," which meant I would have to transfer and never show my face. Ultimately, I decided to walk through, mind my business, and go about my day. While I was walking, someone decided to trip me. Outnumbered, I couldn't do what I wanted to do, so I turned around, ice grilled them, and continued walking. Thinking that everything was over, I kept it moving. Then someone tapped me on the back. While turning around, I was met with a knuckle sandwich. Sticking my left foot out, knees slightly bent, with my hands up, I was ready to defend myself. As with most cowardly groups, the entire group started rushing toward me. While backing up in the middle of Forty-Ninth Street, I kept swinging and trying to grab one of them to get a little revenge. At this time, I was still boxing. Unbothered by the punches, I laughed the entire time. Me getting jumped was nothing in comparison to sparring sessions at Starrett City Boxing Gym. As I entered the building, I dropped my book bag, begging security to let me fight one-on-one. I yelled, "Y'all mad soft. Shoot the fair one. Take turns. Let me fight the leader. Call your OG." Our security guard was a dude named "Gillette." He was a reformed street guy who worked security. I pulled him aside and asked, "Please lock me in a room with one of them." He replied, "Shorty, you've got to chill. Not in front of the staff. Talk to me after school." I asked the leader if he wanted to do a few rounds, but he declined. Curtis, who was a senior training at my gym, warned the gang about me. While meeting with the administration, I'd done what my mother trained me to do—go crazy. The sharpest object in the assistant principal's office was a butter knife. I grabbed it and rushed toward the group. Next, I began whispering to myself for a more dramatic/psychotic effect. My behavior led to an extended suspension. I couldn't deny the infractions, as the administrative team was present the entire time. These tactics were taught to me by my mom for self-defense. Long story short, the leader asked me to be a part of their group. How pathetic. Of course, I declined and reminded him that there was always an open invitation to put on the gloves.

In training children to be independent, it's important to understand adolescent social norms. You must be aware of your surroundings at all times. There are moments when you can't help but protect yourself. I do not support violence, but I do believe in protecting yourself when necessary. If I hadn't spoken up to those bullies during my freshman year, I would have been bullied for the rest of my high school career. Defending oneself does not always imply fighting. Defense might often entail avoiding issues, being cautious about how you joke around, and constantly displaying a stern posture. You cannot be the school's class clown and expect not to have conflicts. An additional lesson learned is the importance of being respectful of one's environment. Crossing the street is sometimes necessary. Doing so isn't an indication of cowardice but intelligence. When visiting my mother, I still acknowledge the local drug dealers and gangsters in my hood. My mother may need their help when I am not present. The other day my mother needed to get help with the groceries. Who helped her? The same guys who are notorious for crime in the community. They hold to specific ancient codes of respecting women and children. For that reason, I do not alienate myself from such people.

Walking Home

Traveling to and from school is a sensitive topic that has long-lasting consequences. Students must be strategic when leaving school, going to the store, deciding what color clothes to wear, who to acknowledge, and who to ignore. Making the wrong decision can be fatal. Though complicated, there are ways of navigating their terrain safely.

The time you leave school is crucial to your journey. In the 9th grade, I didn't follow the codes of traveling. Desperate for attention and trying to fit in, I threw my intellect to the wind. I resided in Brooklyn and went to school in Manhattan; my trip was approximately forty-five minutes. Traveling to school wasn't my issue; it was the return home. My best friend was always on time to leave in the morning. Mornings were calm, being that everyone in our neighborhood attended local schools (South Shore, Jefferson, and Canarsie). The train's swaying felt like its own version of melatonin on trips to Times Square. My internal clock usually went off around the Thirty-Fourth Street station. Missing our stop meant having to go to Seventy-Second or Ninety-Sixth, which felt like a different world.

When going home, I abided by all street codes. I'd wait for friends to get out of school, and in unison, we walked thirty deep to the station. Yelling, screaming, and frightening people at the local Blimpie's was our daily routine. But in the middle of it all was me, the ring leader. Clout and notoriety compromised everything my mother taught me. In hindsight, I pity the straphangers who rode the train with us. We would steal Bon Ton chips, Linden cookies, and quarter waters from local delis. On several occasions, we could have lost our lives, but God's grace covers babies and fools. There was a time that my folly caught up to me.

While fighting Park West High School rivals, I was stabbed in the back of my leg with a kitchen knife. I guess a little context would help. The day started like most others. We waited with one another after school in front of the building. My friends usually walked ahead as I escorted my girlfriend to her train station. She lived uptown. My friends and I had one rule: no one leaves until everyone gets on the downtown one or nine train on Forty-Ninth Street. After dropping my girl off, I noticed my boys had gotten into an argument with students from Park West. Park West High School was right across the street on Fifty-First Street and Tenth Avenue. The origin of the conflict was unclear. As a loyal soldier, I ran into the crowd to fight. Words were being exchanged. I said to myself, "Forget that"—I was swinging first and asking questions later. Being a son of Brownsville, I had been conditioned to understand body language and engage accordingly. I punched someone in the face to commence the ceremony. Adrenaline mixed with dopamine surged throughout my body.

Fighting was quite fun because of training at Starrett City. A royal rumble ensued at the corner of Eighth Avenue and Fiftieth Street. While fighting, a guy from Park West thought swinging a baseball bat would scare me away. No sir. I gave him a classic combo: double jab, right hand, and a left hook. During the chaos, I saw a group stomping a friend. I went to help him out. Someone walked behind me and punched the back of my left leg. "That's odd," I thought. Who would hit me in the leg? I took a few steps, and my body felt strange. Reaching to see what was wrong, I felt warm liquid dripping from the back of my fake Karl Kani denim. Adrenaline subsided as the wound began widening. In a state of shock, I nervously laughed in disbelief. My friends gathered around me on the ground as the Park West students ran off. I laughed the entire time and also in the hospital. I laughed until my mother came. Her words and tears held my heart in suspense. "You are like this because of me being a failure as a parent," she cried. "Eventually, you will be dead or in prison like your father, and there is nothing I can do," she added. As she spoke, my head was permanently affixed to the ground in shame. A failed gangster without the heart to face his mother, I felt stupid. In retrospect, the stabbing was long overdue, considering my behavior. I promised her and myself that was the last time I would bring tears of sadness to my mother's eyes.

There is a laundry list of prerequisites for safely walking home from school. First, do not wait for an entire crowd to walk home. You will adopt the conflicts of everyone walking with you. Rival groups aren't going to stop fighting to ask your specific affiliation to people in your company. Thugs do not perform research and critical analysis before fighting. If you spend time with Crips, you are considered a Crip. Same for Bloods, Patria, Trinitarios, Latin Kings, and so on. Second, students should not be so predictable. People observe your patterns, making it easier to predict your movements. You may not want everyone knowing what time you get out, where you walk, and who you walk with every day.

Differentiating your patterns confuses possible assailants. Once in a while, simply don't be around. Walking with a couple of friends periodically is healthy, but not every single day. Third, fighting other people's battles is for fools. As an educator, I've seen children get hurt protecting friends. This overextended loyalty comes from low self-esteem and wanting to fit in. Loyalty has its place for people who have proved themselves worthy. I wanted to impress my friends and seem tough. There are times you have to help friends defend themselves, but initiating conflicts isn't necessary. Self-defense is reasonable, but that is not what was happening with me. Instead of trying to resolve the issue, I accelerated the skirmish. Often, I think, "What if I would've gotten stabbed in my spine, losing my ability to walk?" If someone asked what happened? My only response would be, "I had to represent for my friends." So ignorant! Sadly, I have friends serving life sentences for the same thing, fighting for friends.

Going to the Store

Entering places of business can be extremely dangerous. The scene with O-Dog and Caine in *Menace II Society* is an example of a worst-case scenario. In the film, once the store owner said, "I feel sorry for your mother," I knew it was downhill from there. My friends and I went to the store together. Our favorite snacks were Little Debbie cakes, quarter waters, and Sour Power. Once in a while, I'd steal quarters from my *abuela*'s purse, which she hid for laundry. We were also masters of stealing. In high school, we became more aggressive, walking out of the store in plain sight of the owners. Sometimes the owners would try to stop us, to no avail.

Walking home from basketball practice, we walked into a store. When my friend Rasheed tried to steal a fifty-cent soda, the clerk grabbed him and swung a shovel at the rest of us. We fought the store owner, throwing juice and pouring chips all over the floor. In retrospect, if the owner had had a gun, someone could've died. To avoid these situations, wait for your friends down the block from the store. You maintain your friendships but avoid possibly dying. Purchasing snacks isn't worth losing your life. Piling into stores to buy food had become a status symbol. In New York City, purchasing bacon, egg, and cheese sandwiches means you're relatively wealthy. I understand the need to seem financially stable, but you have to be smart. If you are entering a store, go with socially responsible friends. If you happen to be in an overcrowded shop, act like someone called your cell phone and walk out. Announcing that you are distraught with the unruly behavior of your peers to the entire crowd isn't necessary.

Clothing, Fits, Gear, Drip

Equally as important as how you travel is what you wear when traveling. Wearing some luxury clothing brands, particularly those associated with celebrity status or gang involvement, is associated with severe peer problems such as theft, assault, and even murder among teenagers. As a result, numerous schools have established dress code standards to limit and prevent such issues (Holloman et al., 1996). Unfortunately, gang life has infiltrated most urban schools. Bloods, Crips, Patria, Trinitarios, MS-13, and a slew of other gangs have engulfed the community. Each gang has customs, traditions, rules, and geographical redlines. For example, in certain areas, wearing red or blue is like asking for death. Also, wearing expensive sneakers and being in the wrong neighborhood is an invitation to be robbed at gunpoint. If you are not aware of these rules, it could cost you your life. Each borough in New York City has a gang territorial map that parents and students should investigate. In addition, the success of local gang-affiliated music artists has increased the number of youngsters recruited.

For this reason, I enforce a dress code in my school. Only business casual attire is acceptable. From my experience, uniforms reduce distractions and increase academic performance. Afterward, they'll have a lifetime to waste money on designer clothes and take selfies on social media. Of interest are parents who spend thousands of dollars on material items while living in poverty. Parents, stop living through your children. Gucci sneakers on a fifteen-year-old child are dangerous and set them up for failure. Adults have to think long term about the impact of their children becoming narcissistic, addicted to material items, and decreasing delayed gratification capacities. Anytime this happens, I blame the parents. They are the ones who buy excessive clothes and create selfish monsters void of modesty.

Black educators, be careful about the impressions you make about clothing in school. Many school districts do not force a specific dress code. Along with kids, I have seen educators wearing expensive name-brand clothing or displaying subtle affiliation to gangs. Our children are watching. We hide behind wanting to be relatable when the truth is that we still hold on to immature behavior, even as professionals. Teach children about marketing, branding, advertisement, and how each industry focuses on Black/Brown communities. We aren't prone to purchasing expensive clothing or gang culture through osmosis. We are apt to follow the trends mentioned earlier through media outlets focused on capitalism and the destruction of our culture. Crip walking, while wearing jays, isn't the core of who we are as a people.

There are daily news reports of teenage killings over material things. Black children are shot for Air Jordans or wearing the wrong colors; it is all the same. Parents and educators must teach children to avoid conflict in every way possible. Students also should avoid the other extreme of "having no swag." Students shouldn't go to the extreme of wearing pants up to their chest, choking their sneakers, and carrying mini-libraries. Balance is key. I can relate to feelings of frustration with having to think of so many nuances of life. Truthfully, your child shouldn't have to undergo such scrutiny just to attend school, but there are social norms in high school that telling our children to ignore will not fix.

Mike's Dirty Little Brother

I grew up in the 1980s to 1990s when name-brand clothes exploded in urban areas. Wearing Tommy, Polo, Nautica, Guess, and other high-fashion clothing lines gave youngsters an assured level of clout. Then entered me, Mike's dirty little brother. I never had the best clothes because our only income was welfare, Section 8, and food stamps. When posted at the pay phone, local drug dealers had rope chains and beepers and carried portable car radios. Girls with Fifty-Four Eleven Reeboks and bamboo earrings weren't concerned with me. Wearing Conway's department store clothes was a repellent to pretty girls. As an adult, I can laugh, but I felt like the biggest loser on earth when I was young. Out of pity, a couple of lowlifes took me to boost from Dr. Jay's in downtown Brooklyn. My best friend let me borrow his old gear because we went to different schools. My favorite pastime was stealing clothes from my older brother Mike. Eventually, his clothes stopped fitting as I outgrew him in the 9th grade. My toes began to cramp when squeezing into his size nine Timberland boots. I wore a size twelve at the time. My mother's unconditional love and words of affirmation provided a little confidence. In her Panamanian voice, she'd said, "Clothes don't make you; you're handsome anyway."

Parents have the power to increase or decrease their children's insecurity and self-esteem. Growing up with a Panamanian mother, who was also a seamstress, was a disguised blessing. My mother never tried to purchase the most expensive clothes for my brothers and me. She regularly preached against materialism. I'd learn it was primarily out of necessity. "Name brands cannot make a person more or less handsome," she'd say. During special holidays she'd sew traditional Panamanian outfits for us. She'd been sewing since the age of ten back home. It only took her one glance at a clothing pattern, and she would create it in hours. On the corner of Franklin Avenue and Eastern Parkway is one of the last Panamanian communities in Brooklyn. After going to the Labor Day parade, she'd show us off to her friends at the local bar. They would stand amazed at our linen outfits, Panamanian gold, and leather sandals. From our culture, we would get praised and then ridiculed when interacting with African American peers. It was a strange experience. Was I cool? Was I not cool? "Who makes the rules?" I thought. Ultimately, I realized "swag" is geographic, regional, and subjective. When I couldn't get new clothes, I wasn't discouraged because I realized the insignificance of such superficial possessions. Parents, be careful about the life lessons you are subconsciously teaching your children.

Research asserts that materialism and conspicuous consumption vary between races/ethnicities—for example, survey data from more than twelve hundred people shows that Black people outperform non-Blacks in materialism and conspicuous consumption (Podoshen et al., 2014). Several parents purchase their children the most expensive material possessions conceivable. Projecting our insecurities to children harms their self-esteem. Used as a symbol of wealth in many Black families, materialism covers our inner turmoil. Being stylish isn't a sin. Our history requires that we get fresh often. Our style and fashion are mimicked internationally. We deserve to enjoy what we've created. Also, some Black students live in dire situations, and having at least one decent outfit goes a long way. I am sensitive to underlying motives, but our children need better financial literacy skills. The price of a sweater can start a company. We have to build up their inner confidence to combat the ever-changing landscapes of society. Using material possessions for false confidence starts them on an endless path. They will never have enough possessions to fill their uncertainties.

Black parents must also model expectations. I have seen grown men spend their entire paycheck on buying clothes to turn up on Instagram. Don't create standards for your children that you do not follow.

Transformative, Revolutionary Educators

Teachers have a difficult time understanding how their actions impact Black children. If teachers subscribe to toxic notions about race, class, and gender, students can be scarred for life. I scarcely recollect my teachers in high school. My relationship with teachers was indifferent. My mother trained me to complete assignments and graduate. Getting in trouble wasn't an option as my mother notoriously dished out spankings. Honestly, my mother rarely hit me when I was younger; it was more of a tongue lashing. As I got older she rarely hit me at all. I received never-ending lectures from her and my aunt about the plight of Black men in America. My dirt was done outside of the school. My teachers repeatedly made it clear their presence was strictly about finances. They were uninterested in building deep, lifelong bonds with students from underserved communities. Subconsciously, I understood that teaching was nothing more than a secure, union-protected job.

New employees need to know that doing the bare minimum will not work. They are to mentor students, participate in extracurricular activities, remember birthdays, and create deep, lifelong, socioemotional connections. No longer will staff be allowed to talk about the mattering of lives without providing evidence of how that concept is expressed in their daily lives outside of their job description. With pride, I can say that my staff understands the importance of going above and beyond for our students. Teachers of all races work tirelessly to support our students.

Race, Diversity, and Inclusion

My high school teachers were from diverse backgrounds. Seeing Black, Latina, white, Jewish, and LGBTQIA community members made learning fun. School was located in Hell's Kitchen, Manhattan, and the staff was a microcosm of the city. The majority of teachers were white liberals. Like most schools, some teachers were dynamic while others put students to sleep. A Spanish teacher wrote all over the board, told us to copy the scribblings, and sat down for the rest of the period. One math teacher was knowledgeable but incredibly dull. He taught algebra, which was my favorite subject, so I'd participate to pass time. Our physical education teacher was by far the meanest. All he cared about was taking attendance on Delaney (attendance) cards and forcing people to sit in the correct floor space. The coolest staff member was the guidance counselor. He was down to earth and honest. He spoke with terms familiar to most Black children. He could discipline us in a way that other teachers could only wish. His leverage wasn't just his similar ethnicity but also his sincere love for students. More than what teachers know, students want to know that teachers *like* them unconditionally. Students excel academically when in nurturing learning environments. Being wanted, liked, and desired immediately changes a student's interactions with teachers. Conversely, being tolerated leads to more tension.

A teacher who developed a fantastic rapport with students when I was in high school was Mr. Becker. Becker was a new humanities teacher. He was a white, out-of-town male, new to the city. Egoless, comfortable laughing at himself and having honest conversations with students. Our old basketball coach retired, and Becker took over. He had no clue how to run plays, train players, or facilitate practice. But he made sure that we had fun. In the middle of games, he'd smirk and say, "Shoot that three-pointer; heck, it might go in." His exaggerated celebrations were the best. A few of his wealthy Wall Street friends came to play ball with us on Saturdays. But when it was time to talk about serious things, we listened to Becker. His race came second to his love for us as students.

Emotional experiences are universal and are significant, if not critical, in academic contexts since emotion influences practically every element of cognition. For example, emotion has a substantial impact on attention, influencing attention selectivity and inspiring action and behavior (Tyng et al., 2017). Students remember how teachers make them feel more than the lessons taught. Students will listen to you more out of their relationship, not because of your title. No one cares about a teacher's titles or degrees. Black students experience horrific violence daily. Treating them with your title means nothing. You cannot scare high schoolers into listening. When a teacher isn't from the community, trying to lecture Black students rarely works. They immediately check the teacher's resume. Listening stops when adults pretend to be something they aren't. So, what is the solution? How do you help students make wise decisions? The answer is simple: relationships. A gentle word from a caring adult can cut through the most callous heart.

Building healthy relationships is just part and parcel of improving outcomes. For example, establishing healthy relationships will not fix a student's poverty, emotional challenges, community tensions, and systemic racism. Instead, they (relationships) lead to conversations that will help students navigate other factors that remain in their lives.

Social-emotional skill development is necessary to building bonds with Black students. Most students live below the poverty line, without both parents, and facing economic problems. First, consider their most immediate needs. They can't learn without basic human needs met. Some students need food, a haircut, books, clean clothes, and so forth, none of which teachers are contractually obligated to purchase. I'd suggest periodically getting these resources for students when possible. If students' basic needs aren't fulfilled, they will not be able to focus academically. Conversely, when their basic needs are met, they can excel in any school setting. Black children aren't intellectually inferior, and they often have extenuating circumstances that compromise their performance.

Additionally, socioemotional intelligence must reside in educators before we can serve students. Unfortunately, some educators devalue this skill because they have been neglected emotionally as children. One cannot pour from an empty cup. If a teacher has personal limitations, their low expectations extend to students.

HURT PARENTS HURT CHILDREN

Research asserts that traumatized parents are more likely to abuse their children, and a PTSD diagnosis or other related trauma in parents is related to child abuse. These correlations appeared to be unrelated to the sort of traumatic incident. Trauma negatively impacts not only the individual but also the family (Montgomery et al., 2019). In addition, parents who experienced trauma as children have trouble meeting the social/emotional needs of their youngsters. Every parent wants their child to excel academically. Families I work with come from low-income communities. They had bad teachers, dropped out, or weren't encouraged to be excellent. Black parents regularly say, "If I didn't do well in school, my mother whooped my behind." To further interrogate that statement, we assume physically abusing children is the best way to support their academic growth. As a result, parents become ineffective at providing support for their children. Yelling, screaming, and physically abusing Black children into submission doesn't produce long-term change. In the past, harsh discipline was temporarily effective. Children weren't as informed as they are now. For instance, my mother often referred to my father's incarceration to straighten me out. "Keep it up, and you'll be just like your father" was her favorite line. My parents regularly used my father's incarceration as a warning. My dad's transparency about his poor decisions was a part of our jail visits. It worked for me temporarily because I had a real-life model. Presently, students are aware that many successful people haven't finished school. Teenagers are becoming millionaires through entrepreneurship on social media. Young people are studying trades such as coding to avoid college. Others are making a fortune by trading sneakers or launching online businesses. The global economy has transformed so much that getting a quality education has become less important. No longer are the only options going to college or being a failure. Scare tactics are ineffective and simply no longer valid. I have students who are wealthier than most educators through marketing on social media and developing their natural talents. So how do parents encourage their children to do well in school with so many distractions?

Teachers and parents have to teach students the historical importance of education for Black people. Black children have never really understood how much their ancestors sacrificed for educational freedoms. From kindergarten, Black children should be informed of the outstanding accomplishments of other nations, not just their own. Different cultures force-feed their distorted histories onto Black children to develop inferiority complexes on our children early. Furthermore, Black children are taught to admire stereotypical roles driven by media. Sports and entertainment aren't our most significant accomplishments as a race. In turn, academic intelligence alienates several Black children from their community. The intellectual heritage of our people should be celebrated more than our prowess in sports and entertainment. Our scholars ought to receive more positive attention in our community. We celebrate former criminals who are released from prison more than students who graduate. While in school, Black scholars receive less attention from the staff. School personnel's concentration is on students with behavioral problems. Educators must prioritize both students according to their needs.

Smart Is the New Gangster

There was a time when being a Black intellectual was applauded in our community. Whether Black Panthers, James Baldwin, Maya Angelou, Nina Simone, Malcolm X, Angela Davis, Afeni Shakur, or Dr. Martin Luther King Jr., these individuals represented the best of us. Presently, our young people believe they can be intelligent or tough, not both. Black children are forced to assume passive, submissive identities to be considered good students. This servile identity is forced on Black children in classrooms and throughout different literary platforms. Black characters in white authors' literature have ascribed a theology of racial submission that calls for a subservient role (Trousdale, 1990). Teachers do not favor assertive Black students; neither do some parents. Confident, powerful, Black children disturb the spirits of some adults. Historically, Black people were praised for being seen and not heard. Presently, young people speak their truths, fighting for social justice and against traditional prejudiced educational systems. Adults have to shift their perceptions of Black intellectualism. It is possible to be a gang member, aggressive, assertive, proud of one's culture, and super intelligent. Black students are capable of academic excellence when permitted to retain their identity. A deeper conversation about these multiple identities must be had within educational circles. Human nature is the singularly labeling individuals, forgetting that humans are complex beings. Our children carry the weight of negative labels that educators often times refuse to transition from. We have all had bad times in our lives, where we made bad decisions. Those isolated incidents do not identify us in totality. Gang participation for some is necessary based on the environment they live in. Many of my students tell me they participate temporarily until they no longer have to.

One of my former students embodies what it means to be an intellectual gangster. He was one of the brightest students I've ever met as an educator. In high school, he was a gifted poet and a phenomenal writer. We spoke periodically about problems he had managing emotions because of family issues. In middle school, he scored high for gifted and talented programs. His parents separated, and he was living with a verbally abusive father. A rough exterior was created to hide inner turmoil. When debating teachers, most of his points were valid. He identified their hypocrisy, lack of intellect, racism, and favoritism in the classroom. Boldly and accurately, he sensed when teachers held grudges. His personality and outspokenness came full circle when he spoke at graduation. His words still resonate in my spirit. To avoid scrutiny from the administration, he submitted a passive, safe, polite speech. While onstage, he changed his first draft to speak from his heart. "I am going to keep it real: this whole thing is fake. I went to school for twelve years, and very rarely saw representation of myself. We push state exams on kids, and never teach financial literacy," he said. I do not remember the speech fully, but I recall first feeling embarrassed, then very proud. He spoke not only for himself but also for other Black children who felt unheard.

It's essential that we allow young Black people to be unapologetic about their identity. Demonizing students for not adhering to submissive roles negatively impacts their performance. Educators and parents have to set aside their pride. Their tone or attitude shouldn't distract us from hearing their hearts. Most of our energy shouldn't be directed toward how the message is communicated. Instead, we must focus on the content of the message. In addition, when youngsters correct us, we should acknowledge our faults. At times, my pride, arrogance, and insecurity made exchanges with young Black people tense. I thought, "They need to be quiet and do as they are told." Subconsciously, I subscribed to an Americanized educational system of oppressive behaviors. I was transferring institutionalized worldviews on children instead of valuing their voices. Undoubtedly, I believe in discipline and structure, but there are methods to support students to develop.

Oftentimes, teachers, parents, and educational leaders focus solely on a child's behavior and rarely hold themselves responsible. If a student curses at a teacher, do we ever ask, what made the student that angry? What type of rapport does the child have with the teacher? What is the child hearing at home? Is this a cry for help and attention? But in reality, we suspend the student, put them in special education, or transfer them to another school. This way of engaging students stems from educators' preconceived notions of the emotional capacity of Black children. We think they should suffer under any condition and then come to school with a smile on their face every day. Unaddressed trauma always bears fruit. Our children are attending schools that hold them to high expectations without adequate resources, whereas other schools have low expectations and their teachers have a limited view of their abilities.

Ineffective Professional Development, Teachers Who Hate Learning

I've attended a fair share of professional development sessions dedicated to forcing educators to improve their pedagogical practices with Black children. When training happens, the people passionate about learning participate the most, while others secretly oppose every research-based point. Most training feels like a waste. Naively, I assume educators will want to provide better service to Black students. Admittedly, I am far from the best educator on earth. Nevertheless, I understand my growth's impact on children, so I try to improve my practice. I have an ancestral obligation, which supersedes my job description.

The Soft Racism of Low Expectations

Low expectations of students stem from one's narrative. White females represent approximately 75 to 80 percent of the teaching force (Loewus, 2017). Relationships between white females and Black people have been negative for the most part. Black bodies were placed six feet underground as the result of lies about the interactions between these two groups. Blacks have been hanged, shot, killed, and mutilated based on the fabricated lies of white women. White female tears equal Black suffering. This is due to the fact that white tears have the power to silence racial minorities (Phipps, 2021). Conversely, white female teachers of Black children face almost impossible conditions. What should they do if they have good intentions, but nationally droves of white women are calling police to kill Blacks for (driving, walking home, jogging, sleeping in their homes, delivering food, playing music, standing on their porch, selling cigarettes, smiling, remaining silent, talking, eye contact, lack of eye contact, etc.)? Childish Gambino's verses show that having cell phones for protection hasn't worked. In his song "This Is America," he points out the many instances where cell phones have been used to film or even live stream at police shootouts and riots, raising questions about violence against African Americans (Winten, 2018). Can you imagine being a Black student having a healthy relationship with a white educator after seeing such images on the internet? They are supposed to assume that white teachers have their best interests in mind even though everything in media says otherwise. Let me qualify my analysis by saying, I am personally familiar with several outstanding white female/male educators. As a student, teacher, and administrator, I have come across some of the kindest white folks one could ever imagine. When I was an assistant principal, a white female staff member adopted a Black student because she was being abused at home. The first person to support me in becoming an administrator was white. However, those instances are few and far between. Those individuals I mentioned regularly address their issues with racism regardless of their good deeds. They are reflective educators who don't come across as if they have arrived. Blaming every negative academic outcome of Black children on one racial demographic isn't wise.

The presidential election of 2016 has also taught me something about how Latinos view Black folks. For clarity, I do not consider myself a Republican, Democrat, conservative, or liberal. Both parties care very little about radically changing the lives of Black folks. But you'd have to be insane to vote for certain candidates. This book isn't about politics; therefore, I will get back to my original thoughts about Latinos and Black people. Trump's votes from Florida were mainly in part due to the Latino population. According to NBC News exit polls, Trump received approximately 55 percent of the Cuban American vote in Florida, while 30 percent of Puerto Ricans and 48 percent of "other Latinos" voted for him (Sesin, 2020). Most conservative Latinos agree with his policies and political views. Some desire to detach from any semblance of the African heritage. Their attitudes transmit into their interactions with Black students. Some Latino educators that are unaware of their origins have a negative view of Black students. Coming from an Afro-Latino household, I have some understanding of where the conflict lies. Many Latinos see whiteness and the edifice of white supremacy as a vehicle for upward mobility. A lighter-skinned minority has the possibility of "passing" as white.

Furthermore, their yearning to pass is in alignment with a need to separate from all traits of Blackness. Passing is a deception that allows a person to adopt roles or identities from which they would be barred by prevailing social standards if not for their deceptive behavior. In the United States, the classic racial passer has been the "white Negro": an individual whose physical appearance allows him to present himself as white, but whose Black lineage qualifies him as a Black under dominant racial rules (Kennedy, 2001). Some will boldly say, "I am Spanish; I am not Black." I have had students tell me that their parents would disown them if they married a Black person. My Afro-Latino mother was shunned by my father's European-Latino family. She was too dark. Colorism and self-hate drive many Latinos to disown their African roots as much as they possibly can. An introductory study of the African diaspora might solve everyone's internal conflicts.

How does this play out in the classroom for Latino teachers and Black students? In many cases, the detachment is subtle and barely noticeable. I have worked in schools in which Latino teachers are especially sensitive to Latino children. *"Mi corazón,"* *"mi hijo,"* *"mi hija,"* *"mi amor"* is heard from teachers to Spanish-speaking students. Black students hear, "Hello, Jamal Smith," "sir," "miss," and so forth. That subtle interaction communicates, "We are not family." I have seen how they interact with Black families of children who are behavioral problems. There is shortness and rigidity that I do not see with Latino children committing similar offenses. Subtle harshness communicates, "I will deal with you, I have to tolerate you, but know for certain that I do not like you." Black children are tolerated, not celebrated like their Latino peers. When students see the difference, they tune out and stop trying to engage academically.

The same is true for Latino children who face similar issues with educators of different ethnicities. From my experiences, Latino students' lack of knowledge of the language and legal status in the country lead to them being submissive. Students have told me their main job in school is to avoid causing any problems that would bring attention to their home. The images of overfilled detention centers have caused many Latino families to be blindly compliant when in schools. There is an increased sensitivity for Latino children compared to Black children. Even in the Latino community, lighter-skinned children are treated better than dark-skinned children. A Latino student from Argentina with Eurocentric features has a very different experience than a Latino student from Panama with African features. Additionally, staff members feel frustrated that immigrant children are compliant, while Black children who have been here since birth are "disruptive." Black children are now becoming a minor minority in the educational system.

LATINOS, EMBRACE YOUR BLACKNESS

Most Hispanic people do not identify with their African roots. A Pew Research Center survey of Latino adults shows that one-quarter of all US Latinos self-identify as Afro-Latino, Afro-Caribbean, or African descent with roots in Latin America (Afro-Latino Report, 2016). Knowing your entire history as a Latino changes how you view Black children. Do a little research and set yourself free. I understand the fear of admitting to the world you're Black. Latinos loving Black culture publicly can feel like a death sentence. Often, people are disowned for dating a Black person. But you have to make clear boundaries and decisions for your life. Being ashamed of your heritage will negatively impact your performance as an educator.

Black Educators Who Dislike Black Children

Because of my bias, I don't like publicly admitting the faults of my people. But, in the spirit of objectivity, I have to make it plain. Oftentimes, Black children are disappointed the most by Black educators. Black teachers can become forgetful of their culture and ashamed of who they are and hate everything Black children do. This overseer, house Negro paradigm has historical implications. Plantation owners started hiring Negroes to keep the field Negroes in line. A Black overseer manufactured the worst whippings for his master. He would do so to keep his position as the most trustworthy, obedient, docile Negro on the property. This behavior continues in our schools.

There is always that one Black educator who tries best to be the strictest disciplinarian in the building in order to show white counterparts they're in command. Utterly pathetic. Most have lost self-respect, imitating the actions of their oppressor. They see a path to getting recognition and being accepted by white society, though they never will. Throughout my time as a student, teacher, and administrator, I have seen all of these characters come to life. To my shame, earlier in my career, I was the loud, obnoxious Negro, keeping others in the line. I didn't realize that I was being used to perpetuate the myth of the magical Negro, similar to Joe Clark.

Solutions: SAY IT LOUD, BE PROUD

Historically, change comes by way of force. As Black educators, we must boldly display our love for our people. Publicly celebrate your culture. Turn to brothers/sisters in the building and plan events, diversify your instruction, provide culturally relevant materials. Get into good trouble. Because of current events, it is the best time to be aggressive. Also, know that you will never be accepted. No matter how you try, the body you are wrapped in will not change. Love who you are, unapologetically.

10TH GRADE

The 10th grade is a time of settling in and reconnecting with your tribe. Over the summer, many Black upcoming sophomore children have a "coming to Jesus" moment. They view high school differently, and maturity kicks in. The guild of being relaxed and seeming unbothered takes over.

After 9th grade, everything seemed different to me. Everyone grew, people were in serious relationships, and getting new clothes was more important than playing street fighter. Calculations for graduating with forty-four credits and five Regents became real. Problematic students begin realizing time was running out.

To avoid seeming unintelligent, some misbehave even more in an attempt to be expelled. Others regularly fight to create an illusion that the entire world is stopping them from being scholars. Sports, extracurricular activities, and other staples of school life further complicate things. You have to start listening to adults and making efforts to graduate.

Friendship selection becomes more crucial to success, and students begin ending lifelong friendships. Shared special occasions throughout elementary, middle, and high school start coming to a close. Students have to make difficult choices. Do I remain friends with someone who I know is a distraction? Do I choose friends who are helping me? I have seen this play out for several of my students, and it's more complicated than you think. This transition has several nuances and layers that few people discuss. Geographic, emotional, and sometimes spiritual ties are cut.

Students typically join gangs or interact with specific individuals to demonstrate their great allegiance to their neighborhoods. The presence of gangs is nevertheless quite disruptive to the normally tranquil school environment. When kids lack a sense of belonging or acceptability in their lives, gang affiliation takes hold in a school; for example, recent immigrants join gangs to maintain a strong ethnic identity (Burnett & Walz, 1994). Consider students in the 10th grade who live in the same projects. They have been walking to and from school together for over a decade. They've fought against other neighboring projects with one another, seen close friends die, and so forth. Being together is more than friendship; they are family. Two young men knew each other from infancy. Both were street kids from good homes. One had learning disabilities he concealed through cutting class and fighting. I could see through it. The other was academically sound but embarrassed to let friends know. Teachers would talk about how smart he was, and students would mention the gang wars he was in around the neighborhood. One day the secret scholar shared his fear. He said, "Who would I walk home with? Who would be my friend?" He continued, "I wouldn't be able to go outside because all of my friends are in the streets." I encouraged him to box, play basketball, and do anything to keep himself busy.

Sports guys usually got a pass. Ultimately, he could not stomach the pressure. He cut class and smoked marijuana even more. Seeing him broke my heart. Once, I saw him cutting class and smoking across the street on Dekalb Avenue. I asked, "Have you given up?" With a nervous smile, he replied, "To be honest, yes. I just can't do it." This inability to stand firm against peer pressure happens to a lot of young Black children. They sincerely want to be successful but lack resources to stand alone. The consequences of bad peer/tribe selection are delicate for Black children. Adults must continue supporting their efforts.

Solutions for 10th Graders

Encourage them to select peers who willingly challenge their character. Several of our children explore their immediate environment/community. Traveling to another neighborhood is a big deal for them. We have to expose children to different places. And exposure doesn't necessarily mean vacations. Vacations don't necessarily give them an understanding of life outside of their community. Parents and educators have to show students that it is possible to live differently. Visit affluent Black communities, historically Black colleges, and their countries of origin. Doing so gives them a global view of the world. They leave knowing their small block doesn't represent all of humanity. Children living in urban settings need time to connect with nature, fresh air, and open spaces. As students come back to the classroom, they are more relaxed and prepared to learn. If they cannot travel, at least have them spend time in different peer groups. They should see that hanging with "jocks" is just as cool as spending time with "nerds." Differentiate students' experiences, and exposure to new communities will transform their view of the world.

Exposing teenagers to diverse peer groups is crucial to their social development. Adults, reassure students that Blackness is not a monolith. I always refer my students to revolutionaries who were both intelligent and hip. There are several historical and modern figures to use as a reference. When I was recently speaking with my son, he told me about Tyler the Creator's new album. Usually, I tease him about his music selection. Mumble rappers kind of get on my nerves. When he mentioned Tyler, I was taken aback. When I asked him why, he said, "I like that he is different." "What do you mean?" I asked. He continued, "He chose to have his own flow, style, and delivery. Also, he is super intelligent, but he isn't cocky." There is a long list of people whom we can direct our Black children to study. As adults, we have to be familiar with their interests.

Mentoring is Essential

Research suggests that Black students in mentoring programs have considerably higher academic attainment scores and academic achievement than their nonmentored counterparts. Furthermore, racial identity attitudes of immersion and internalization and affiliation with academics were found to be substantially related to standardized achievement assessments and GPA (Gordon et al., 2009). When we think of mentors, people often think of Big Brother and Big Sisters of America. These are phenomenal programs that have changed the lives of several young people. However, when I think of mentoring, I think of the power of peer mentoring. Research indicates that peer mentoring programs decrease student dropouts, irrespective of socioeconomic status (Sprague, 2007). As students start to form tribes, there is always one person everyone knows is the alpha, the person who reminds the group about the importance of going to class, doing work, and so forth. Peer mentors can help students more effectively than adults.

I remember having difficulty with a student and utilizing a peer mentor. A student was stealing all the MacBooks from a laptop cart. We had a novice teacher from the suburbs who was not familiar with Brooklyn. We had protocols for securing laptops. He subconsciously ignored the procedure and just let the kids take computers freely. He was an excellent teacher engrossed in his lesson, losing sight of classroom behaviors. He was doing projects and experiments, and the kids were in the class. While this was happening, one of my students was taking laptops home to resell. By the time we did inventory, ten computers were missing. As with all teenagers, someone told on him. When I questioned the student, he chose to remain silent, denying all allegations. Usually, when this happens, students start cursing as a distraction to get suspended. Instead of continuing the questioning, I turned to an alpha student.

I wasn't sure if he was selling drugs or sticking people up, but everyone knew the alpha was about that life. For some reason, as is the case most times, he was super respectful in school. He would say, "Yes sir and yes ma'am" to everyone who crossed his path. He never got into fights and barely cut class. Side note for educators: kids who are really in the street rarely cause trouble in school. They have enough happening in their personal life. School becomes a refuge of peace. Maybe he was on parole or had an open case. Either way, he was never a problem. I tapped him on the should at lunch and told him about the situation. I said, "Listen, man, I do not want to get the police involved; just tell your people to give up the laptops." He looked at me with a smirk and said, "I got you, Mr. B." The following day, magically, the computers turned up. Not one was missing. The alpha walked up to me and asked, "Everything good?" At that moment, I realized that our students have more power than us as educators. I've sought out influencers in everything that I have worked on ever since.

ALPHA STUDENTS

Peer mentoring has been effective at improving academic outcomes. Students can motivate one another differently than adults. Valuing and respecting a person's voice has more to do with connection than age. In our school communities, there are students (alphas) who garner the respect of peers. The term "alpha" refers to a dominant person or their behavior, particularly in socially aggressive, hypermasculine individuals. We may criticize the students who have high social status, but they have the attention of the student population nonetheless. Honoring what the students value provides an opportunity for dialogical conversation. From sports stars to street kids, each character has worth. When we respectfully engage alphas, they rarely push back.

Students are alphas in different areas of their lives. Some are leaders in sports, while others are academic alphas. I had a team of alphas in different areas who helped me. As a 10th grader, my peers had the most significant positive impact on my growth. Friends woke me up for school, ensured that my homework was complete, and stopped me from getting into fights. Relatively immature, I was still trying to live out Wu-Tang videos. Scared, dazed, and confused, I was hell-bent on fitting in. One friend who was an excellent student/athlete encouraged me to play basketball. Sadly, I was decent at best and never took the sport seriously. Childhood friends such as J.R., Taquan, Anthony, Gregory, Seneca, and Stretch were destined for the pros, not me.

I was decent at ball handling, passing, rebounding, and using my body to bully people. Being a lefty made things easier for me offensively. People kept forgetting. Tryouts were exciting. I used what I learned from boxing to improve in basketball. In boxing, developing a decent jab can take a year. I worked day in and day out with my friend Seneca. He wasn't serious about ball at the time, but he could shoot from anywhere. Hand down, man down. At tryouts, I went off. I grabbed boards, pushed the ball, and dished it to shooters. For my size, my speed caught people off guard. Seneca would spot up as soon as I grabbed it off the backboard. Ultimately, I made the team and became the captain. Playing ball kept me out of trouble in the neighborhood. Another friend encouraged me to go to church. In all honesty, I was chasing a girl, and I got stuck in the congregation. The church gave me a firm foundation and a community of people attempting to live righteous lives. I started in the 10th grade, and I am still attending almost thirty years later. I credit peers with transforming my life. I'd heard several positive quotes from older family members, but I understood them better from friends for some reason.

Village Mentality

The African proverb "It takes a village to raise a child" reveals a deeper reality. Most societies around the world do not expect moms or parents to raise their children on their own. Instead, mothers and their young children are typically integrated into broader kinship groups and communities that assist with childcare and other responsibilities (Seymour, 2013). Surrounding our children with a village ensures their academic/socioemotional success. Surround them with people willing to have authentic dialogue. As a parent, I get weary of repetitive conversations with my children. I encourage them to speak to people they hold in high regard and inform me afterward. If I am wrong, I humbly accept my correction. Not having a village can be fatiguing. Frustrated parents often surrender, losing to negative entities.

Parents become too liberal, too soon with high schoolers. In freshman year, parents are super involved. They come up to parent-teacher conferences and PTA meetings, communicate with teachers, and so on. Once their child is in the 10th grade, they believe the work is complete, and their children can raise themselves. Parents, however, should be more attentive as children age. The parental expectation being communicated doesn't equate to perfect execution by children. My son mocks me when I lecture him about my upbringing. Preaching to him has no effect. My entire household is dog tired. My strategy has altered. Presently, I ask them to express their thinking and provide subtle, nonabrasive suggestions.

Effectively communicating parental expectations varies for each child. I spoke with a parent whose daughter was misbehaving, cutting class, fighting, and so forth. The parent persistently forced the daughter to complete school assignments. After the daughter participated in a fight, the parent and I proposed that she write a letter apologizing to all students. They read short essays discussing the negative impact of violence. Anytime I called the parent, she came to the school immediately. She didn't defend or justify her child's behavior. She fully supported any disciplinary actions I took toward her child. She remained steadfast during meetings and cried when her daughter left the room. Soft at the core, the mother wanted her daughter to avoid her mistakes as a youngster. Ultimately, the child was a few credits shy of graduating and attended a transfer school. The student graduated later than usual but finished nonetheless. Presently, the daughter is in college, and the mother works as a teacher in my school.

LAZY PARENTING

Young people are aware of their parents' expectations, and parents communicate their values subconsciously. If your child does poorly in school and then receives new video games, you are telling children that school does not matter. The American educational system hates the existence of Black children. Therefore, many misbehave to avoid being in a place set on their failure. Believing what a teacher says about your child without a conversation is naïve. Special education and suspension centers are full of children of docile parents who choose not to be objective listeners. Parents, be wary of assuming your child is wrong. Think critically and listen to your child. If you aren't present, do not overreact. Ultimately, the example we set as parents guides their actions.

Research indicates that parent-child and parent-school participation positively influence student attitudes/actions, indirectly affecting student achievement (Wilder, 2014). Regardless of a parent's socioeconomic status, their involvement in school-related activities positively impacts student performance. Also, excelling in our fields of expertise is the most potent lecture a parent can give. We cannot all be doctors and lawyers. A job title isn't what makes a parent an example worthy of imitation. Taking your job and role as a parent is good enough. A close friend's parents are examples of professionalism. Her parents are immigrants and raised three college-educated children who are financially stable and prosperous. The father wakes up early every morning, irons his clothes, packs lunch to save money, and is a highly professional security guard. Financially, he saved enough to help each child when they were first married. The parents share metro cards, pay rent on time, and regularly have family dinner. Her mother takes care of homes for a living. Similar to her husband, she's at work on time and professional. The parents also held their children to a high level of excellence. All three children were trained to take academics seriously. In turn, they all completed college on time. All children are successful professionals and now take care of their parents.

In contrast, research shows that familial socioeconomic status (SES) stratifies some of the benefits of parental participation. For example, Black families living in poverty or low-income communities will have additional issues compared to others. To mediate and overcome SES challenges, parents are encouraged to maintain high academic expectations, provide ongoing parental support for child learning, have parent-child discussions of school matters, participate in school governance/events, and read together to impact student achievement positively (Tan et al., 2020).

Invest in Your Children

Our children are our most significant investments. At some point, they will be caring for us, providing shelter, and taking us to doctor's appointments. Life is a cycle. How we raise them now will impact how they care for us later. Unfortunately, some parents feel unable to call children to heights we haven't reached. We feel hypocritical, and to an extent, we should. If we tell children they have to become world-class surgeons, yet we've never been to medical school, something's wrong. Their greatness doesn't revolve around our expectations. We should inspire our children to be great, but we cannot force them. My greatest joy is watching my children surpass me. My mother regularly said, "Do as I say, not as I do," humbly admitting that she wasn't the best example to imitate. She also warned me by saying, "Follow me if you want; just know that I will not be saving you." Quality parenting doesn't require perfection. It requires humility. The reason I sincerely love my mother is that she was/is humble about her flaws. I can never hold a grudge about what I didn't have growing up because she was transparent about her shortcomings.

Some of our children grow to hate us because we lie about who we are, and once they figure out the truth, they become bitter.

The same is true for educators' expectations of students. It's interesting to watch educators use fear as a teaching strategy. I've said things like, "Why don't you focus?," "Stop being a follower," and "Be your own person" to students and my children. Me?! The kid who had the weakest spine on earth? The kid who joined gangs out of fear? Really. I am a poor man's Joe Clark who got a little title, and now I want to give inspirational speeches. Educators, stop frontin.' We are far from perfect, and our students see through us. Please keep it one hundred. Some of us barely made it out of college and got our jobs because of social connections. Others cheated in high school, on SATs, had other people write papers in college, and graduated with a degree we didn't earn. Now you're deconstructing *Between the World and Me*? Yeah, okay. As an administrator, I have seen teachers fail students for coming late to school while they have been written up about their own tardiness. Other teachers wanted children suspended for fighting another student while they themselves got into a public argument with another staff member. Students have a sixth sense of hypocrisy, and it drives them crazy to be around fake people.

Pacifying Adult Children

Having a parent in prison and one who relies on public assistance created a fight-or-flight mentality within me. My mother made it clear that if I didn't take care of myself, no one else would either. What's become increasingly problematic is financially unstable parents pacifying their children into their adult years. My brothers and I had to graduate from high school, be in college, work by eighteen, or leave my mother's apartment. The rules were objective and consistent for all of us.

Teens are entitled, spoiled, self-centered, and resistant to hard effort. Despite putting forth little effort, they expect to win at everything. They don't foresee any consequences for their selfish behavior. They are more concerned with obtaining comfort and pleasure than establishing a meaningful living for themselves in the future. Perhaps the parents of these teenagers tried too hard to compensate for the harsh parenting they had themselves as children. Maybe they were neglected as children and are so lacking in self-esteem that they go to their children for validation (Sirota, 2017). Currently, I see parents buying designer clothes for unemployed adult children. This mixed message about expectations confuses children and will eventually burn out parents. Traumatized Black parents overcompensate for their loss. Children of single parents, who become parents, overcompensate by developing unhealthy attachments to their children. For myself, not having a father around makes me overbearing as a parent. I get worried about everything, I can be super sensitive, and I fear harming them in any way. Over time I have learned that making mistakes is also a part of being a great parent. My job is to try to be my best, not perfect.

I'm tempted to give my children everything I wanted as a kid. For me, wearing hand-me-downs was depressing, especially in the housing project where the dozens were a part of life. "Yo, look at Mike's dirty little brother Shawn wearing his old pants!" friends would yell out. Never wanting my kids to feel such embarrassment, I splurge now and then. Purchasing gift for your kids periodically is an excellent form of positive reinforcement. Conversely, undeserving children receiving rewards is poisoning their character. Receiving twenty-fifth-place *effort* awards creates a sense of entitlement. Be comfortable saying no when you have to.

Kids Are Always Watching

Arguing with educators in front of children communicates a dangerous message. I've witnessed parents cursing out teachers in front of their children. Just yesterday, a parent cursed me out because of an Instagram beef between her child and another student. Children then do the same when parents aren't present. Their respect for authority figures dissolves instantaneously. School discipline no longer has value in their mind. To clarify, there are moments when one must speak with a firm tone to staff. Verbal and physical abuse should never be tolerated. As a parent, I confront my children's teachers regularly. For example, the other day, I talked with my daughter's after-school monitor. Another girl hit her over a crayon. I firmly stated, "This can never happen again. I expect to be contacted in the future, and both students need to have a mediation session." I then informed my daughter in front of the monitor that she is a Black queen who is not to be physically harmed by anyone, not even me. Each confrontation is done with respect. I want my child to speak with confidence and be respectful. Parents, are you preparing your child to deal with conflict in a healthy manner when you aren't present? What do they see when you are home with your spouse? Have you subconsciously taught your children to either shut down or explode when angry?

My lessons in dealing with conflict came through boxing. My concept of boxing was based on fights I'd seen growing up in Brownsville. I thought people in the ring were archenemies who would kill one another if given the opportunity. This is not the case. After every sparring match, sportsmanship rules demand that opponents shake hands. When I first started, I'd be close to tears and wanting to curse out my sparring partner. I was taught to detach emotions from physical pain in the gym. The same is true for parents and students in school. We (parents) are to be examples at all times. Once a parent starts cursing and yelling at teachers, their children are doomed.

When parents behave that way toward me as a principal, I shake my head and apologize to the student. Children are so utterly embarrassed each time it happens. The insecurity of having to figure out adulthood from such a poor example is obvious.

Parenting issues and tensions are quickly resolved when parents have an honest dialogue with their children. Unfortunately, most students don't speak transparently with parents about school. They choose to be silent after constantly being unheard. During my career, students' expressiveness has decreased significantly. A part of the problem for teens is their overuse of cell phones and cell phone addiction. Unfortunately, this phenomenon is wreaking devastation on their relationships and mental and emotional well-being (Lee, 2021). Beside cell phone addiction, teens choose not to communicate because parents do not listen. Contrary to what parents believe, students desperately want to share their truths. However, harshness and unrealistic adult standards tell them to be quiet. As a parent and educator, I've had to ask myself, "Do I care to listen to young people speak?" When I was disagreeing with my son Junior (fifteen years old), he clearly articulated that I wasn't open to listening. He said, "You ask me questions, then predict what I am thinking or make a face indicating that what I say is a lie. You don't care about listening, just being heard."

Many educators do not care to listen to teenagers either. They are too consumed with getting through a curriculum, teaching outdated content, and abusing their authority. Instead, some use students' vulnerability to threaten and shame them during a future conflict. For Black students, teachers' listening skills diminish even more. Last week a Black student in another school was having a rough day and just needed to stop out in the yard to take a break. Instead, he was met with safety agents arresting him. He expressed his emotions and was arrested as a result. This is an example of the world that Black children live in. No one wants to hear them out. Parents and educators only want their full compliance.

Passing the Torch (Black Trauma)

It's human nature to transfer culture, traditions, and history. Cooking recipes and inspirational stories of old are healthy and needed in the Black community. When we go in the wrong direction, we continue negative patterns. Violence becomes normalized. We say, "My momma used to whoop me!" with a grin. For getting kids' attention, we reason the belt is the best tool. Violence as a form of communication stems from our experiences when enslaved. Paulo Freire states, "The oppressed, instead of striving for liberation, tend themselves to become oppressors" (Freire & Macedo, 2018). Hurt people hurt people. Blacks harm one another as the result of four centuries of torture. Abuse isn't a "Black" way of parenting; it's what has been conditioned into our ethos. Parents, be wary of extending trauma from your family's heritage to your children. Consider the origin of your parental paradigm.

During slavery, Black parents could not be openly affectionate or patient with their children if they made mistakes. There was no time, as the environment did not permit soft parenting skills. Physical abuse was used out of desperation. It was seen as less harmful than the slaver's whip or the tightening of the rope. Parents couldn't acknowledge their emotional connection to their children, as slavers would use this for manipulation. Disgustingly, Black parents were at times forced to have sex with their children for breeding. If parents spoke positively about their children, the family was immediately separated. Slavers cut off the tongues of Black children heard reading. Black children with talents or intellectual prowess suffered the most.

These parenting strategies persist. Teachers hate "mouthy" children. Outspoken Black children are seen as a "problem." Parents still believe beating children fixes everything. Some parents sincerely do not understand the purpose of affection. The phrase "keeping it real" is utilized to mask lazy, uninformed parental skills. Verbal and physical abuse is not sustainable in the long term. Once your children become adults, what else can be used as a threat? Not much. Internal change happens through dialogue. Parents who focus on internal, long-term behavior improvement have better outcomes with their children. Parents should not focus energy primarily on expressing disapproval. Whatever we place energy into grows. Having balance in parenting is critical to being effective.

Some educators subconsciously enjoy watching Black children get physically assaulted by their parents. On several occasions, I've heard staff members say, "What that boy need is a good butt whooping from his father." In conferences, I have seen staff members use language to push parents to curse students out. Why? Most believe the best way to get misbehaving Black children in line is through a beating. Parents have even verbally abused their children to try to impress me. I usually intervene, letting the parents and teacher know that there are other ways to help a student change.

Effectively Communicating—Words Hurt

According to research in the journal *Child Development*, being too strict, to the point of being harsh—which includes yelling, punching and shoving, and using other verbal and physical threats as punishment—might harm our children's potential to achieve in high school and college (Wallace, 2017). Effectively parenting Black children requires analyzing each scenario and providing appropriate support. We have to avoid extremes. There are many other options besides yelling and remaining silent. Simultaneously, we must discipline intentionally and be gracious when necessary. Admitting fault as a parent is a magic trick few people discuss. Educators exude hypocrisy regularly, and students are left defenseless. Home should be different. Some form of equity should be afforded when home.

Being wrong is humiliating for some parents. My children collectively rejoice when I do something wrong. Jonathan, my son, allows me to lecture and smirks each time I mispronounce a word. My wife has a Rolodex of my failures that she refers to when I become arrogant. I cannot count the times I've accused my children of wrongdoing and then been laughed at when corrected. I love being married to a woman who is willing to be held accountable when necessary. My wife Jennifer is quick to say, "Hey, buddy. I know you're upset now; remember, you've been wrong in the past." It is a quick reminder not to be emotional in the moment. Creating an environment of healthy debate starts with parents.

I remember having to debate with my son about screen time and valuing homework. When the pandemic first began, I became concerned about screen time. He was unable to meet up with friends and stated that video games were his only outlet. Before COVID-19, we did not allow electronics during the school week. Needing additional screen time for socialization was his argument. He cited the necessity of socializing during a pandemic to improve mental health. You have to admit, he's good. Next, he discussed how homework is worthless. "Homework is not proven to increase intellect," he said. He continued, "Less homework gives families more time to interact." After doing research, I realized he was right. Scientists studying the social-emotional impact of the pandemic have encouraged virtual interaction and less extended homework assignments. I apologized; he got me again. Our house rule stands: research and data have the final word in all of our decisions. Children's requests are valued based on research. Objective analysis improves our relationship and humbles us as parents.

Healthy debating at home prepares students for the world. Force-fed parenting hinders critical thinking skills. Our children aren't always "disrespectful" when they have questions. They are intelligent scholars who need quantitative data to draw realistic conclusions. Instead, parents' egos create false narratives. Our children become fearful sheep unable to defend themselves as adults. Courage is developed at home. When educators harm your son/daughter, they won't know how to confront them.

Confronting people is a large part of our parenting strategy. Once, my second son Jonathan felt wronged by a cafeteria assistant. The staff member stated that he was fooling around and raised her voice. I scheduled a meeting with the assistant principal, and Jonathan led the conversation. He was instructed to speak with confidence and make sure his voice was heard. If we are indeed preparing our Black babies to become executives, lawyers, and world-class surgeons, dealing with conflict is a part of the job.

11TH GRADE

The 11th grade is when most students begin preparing for college. Their academic performance is under a microscope. Some Black children become afraid of having to fend for themselves. Many have heard the ultimatum "Get a job, go to college, or get out" from parents. Students who fooled around their entire 9th and 10th grade try repenting in the 11th. Ultimately, 11th graders subconsciously self-fulfill their expectations. Many make the necessary changes as they mature, while others damage themselves academically; turning the tide is almost impossible. A large number of failed courses and unexpected pregnancies make "catching up" difficult. Others join gangs, start smoking, and now have obligations that will not allow time to focus. Under nearly impossible conditions, some students find a way.

When arriving at our school as a freshman from the Dominican Republic, Jose was a terror. He smelled of marijuana and rarely did any schoolwork. I begged him to stay off the streets, but to no avail. He became involved with a local Dominican gang (Trinitarios). Trinis, as they are called, have a higher level of viciousness. Instead of fighting any rivals by shooting them, they use machetes. Jose began receiving death threats as a result of joining. For protection, he got a gun and a machete to boot. Regardless of his behaviors on the street, the staff loved him. Around us, he had a childlike, playful demeanor.

Our staff's relationship with him led to improved academic performance. Peers helped with translating, homework and tutoring. Being a charmer with females helped him a lot. Jose and I started boxing training to stay occupied and release stress. Next, I taught him about cutting hair and DJing parties. Everything was working out, and then his girlfriend became pregnant. The staff knew he would have to work full-time and stop attending. Jose's attendance dropped, and he was standing across the street selling dime sacks. He said, "I'm wasting my time. I have to make money for the baby." I tried to persuade him to do both, but he disagreed. His mother and little brother depended on him financially. He had been forced to be the man of the house at ten years old and now had a baby on the way at sixteen years old. Eventually, he began working construction, and we haven't been able to contact him since. Unfortunately, his story is familiar to professionals in urban education. Michelle Fine shares the many reasons "dropouts" depart early from school. In *Framing Dropouts*, she asserts that students leave school for numerous reasons: getting bored, not getting it, being held back in earlier grades, and being pushed out against their will (Fine, 1991). Many students' life circumstances compromise their performance, as they have little wiggle room for mistakes. The nuanced factors that negatively impact student achievement are of no interest to policymakers. On the other hand, transformational leaders are tasked with creating preventive academic supports.

There are students terrified of remaining in impoverished communities, and they use education to escape. I was one of those students. Educators, parents, and policymakers must figure out how to get Black children to desire academic excellence internally. I suggest providing real-world experiences with diverse populations. The Kauffman Foundation recently commissioned a poll of kids and adults. Participant results show that students graduate from high school college ready, not career ready. According to respondents, "American high schools are not doing enough to prepare pupils for success outside of academic contexts" (Scheidegger, 2019). Financial stability is the desire of most Black children. I was on government assistance my entire childhood. As I considered career options, drug dealers made the most money in Brownsville. Next, boxing legends like Mike Tyson, Riddick Bowe, Shannon Briggs, Daniel Jacobs, and a childhood friend Curtis Stevens. Finally, barbers like Alvin "Satch" were considered local legends.

I started cutting hair at the age of twelve after Aunt Olivia bought clippers. People raised in the projects know that getting a bad cut is like signing one's own death warrant. Friends will crack jokes without pausing for the rest of your life. As a result, I practiced unrelentingly. Mylah's (my female cousin) dolls were used for fades. By the time I was in high school, I had made $10 a cut from friends. I would cut hair on staircases, at my house, anywhere to get a few bucks. Alvin, the barber, gave me an option to imitate. He had a decent-paying job and stayed out of street politics.

Long-term academic goals leave young people disinterested. Expecting children to patiently wait four to six years to see the fruits of academia is unrealistic. What are they supposed to do during that time? What about their immediate needs? Part-time work gives them real-world experiences that improve academic achievement. Employment teaches youngsters soft skills such as punctuality and budgeting, which transfer into their careers. Parents should also tell their kids to make sure that part-time jobs don't become full-time. I've seen students on track to graduate drop out to work at a shoe store. Keep your eye on the long-term goal.

Eleventh graders who struggled in lower grades have the most difficulty finishing on time. The option of dropping out to work is logical if you are poor. Existing in violent, low-income communities, turning down a job to study physics seems irrational. Also, their past inequities still live in the minds of unforgiving teachers. In addition, their parents may have been abusive and emotionally unavailable. As the walls close in, too many students eventually quit.

Immediate Finances versus Long-Term Goals and Solutions

There are many ways educators and parents can help students succeed under challenging circumstances. Counternarratives—stories of people whose lives shatter the fictions of master narratives—appear as vital and perhaps life-saving efforts. Counternarratives are the polar opposite of stories that benefit only a few people's lives (Roberson, 2019). For Black students, educational policymakers enjoy highlighting their deficits and mumbling about their incredible strengths. Everyone should share stories of students who have triumphed from similar backgrounds. Youngsters believe that their narrative is isolated. As a kid, I thought I was the only one on food stamps and had no father at home. Teaching community building reduces shame and embarrassment. Westernized culture believes in competition and isolation. Blacks are now socialized to kill one another over internet rumors—African tradition teaches unity and sharing resources. The media's portrayal of Blacks should be combatted with stories of Black excellence. We should modify our teaching strategies to improve outcomes.

Distance learning has negatively impacted all students, especially Black students. In addition, distance schooling isn't working for many families because of mental health issues, poor internet connections, and fewer childcare options. According to research, kids with impairments, those living in poverty, and Black and Latinx children are most vulnerable to falling behind (Miller, 2021). Racism happens on Zoom calls as well. When I visited classrooms virtually and peeked in on my children, I noticed Black students being corrected more than others. Fully remote virtual learning has lasting negative implications. Misused technology allows students to avoid metacognitive growth. I saw a student take a picture of a math problem and receive the answer without any work done. I asked the student, "Did you know how to get the answer?" "Yes, I just didn't want to do the work," the student replied. A lack of rigorous academic engagement is a danger for Black students. Academic laziness transfers into their personal/professional lives. The pandemic has drained student motivation and created a more significant learning gap. Students must play catch up in preparation for college-level coursework. Their critical thinking skills and logic will need additional remediation. We cannot force our 11th graders to improve in the areas mentioned above. We can only act as consultants as they mature into young adults.

Parenting 11th-grade students is more about advice and less about authoritative discipline. They are independent thinkers. We cannot police their every move. The impact of threats is all but diminished. Parents begin reaping what they sowed when their kids were young. Abusive parenting is revealed to be a farce. Teenagers eventually stop being afraid of parental punishment.

Stubbornly, some parents continue threatening to send children to military school and disowning them. Seeds planted in the hearts of the young begin taking root. Fortunately, countless times I've seen children display tremendous growth because of core values learned at home.

I have a long list of students who gave me headaches as a principal. They are now successful adults. A former student who changed comes to mind. Regularly, I had to chase him out of the hallways, begging him to go to class. When meeting his parents, I was astonished by his actions. It made no sense. His parents were God-fearing, kind people. They apologized for his behavior, asking me not to transfer him. I felt so bad for his parents, and at the same time I related to the student. Everyone goes through a stage trying to figure out life and making bad decisions. He started dating a reserved girl who did well in school and magically got him to improve. "Yo, I gotta go to class; wifey is going to flip," he said to friends. Many students improve as a result of having well-intentioned boyfriends or girlfriends. As stated before, students communicate with their peers more effectively than they do with adults and youngsters. Parents have to be persistent and poised when speaking. Having the support of a village lessens the load.

Extended family and church-based social networks are essential resources for African Americans because they provide instrumental emotional, social, and psychological assistance and resources to their members (Nguyen et al., 2016). My mother was notorious for getting other people to speak with me about my behavior. She would usually call on her girlfriends, my aunt, and my grandmother. When everything failed, she would call my dad in prison. There was no shame in her parenting. She'd use my godmother Millie's gentleness to leave me in tears. Our young people respond well to careful correction. Extended family members have more influence than parents. Relatives and people in the community have social capital with our children. Instead of being defensive, parents should lean on others when necessary. With limited resources, Blacks cannot afford to create an isolated atmosphere where only their words matter. Parents do not live forever. When we are gone, our villages will continue supporting our kids—additionally, parents' worldviews compromise their judgment. Encourage your child to listen to trustworthy adults with diverse viewpoints.

Teachers can transform lives by developing authentic relationships. Every effective teacher I've supervised has had excellent rapport with students. They are magical beings able to motivate the most stubborn student. One such staff member was a guidance counselor. When students were in distress, they ran to her office. Another staff member was born in the community—every student assigned to her advisory graduates on time. Each school has staff members like this. Often, they aren't given their roses while alive. They may not have the instructional abilities or relationship skills with another staff member necessary to gain fame. Then there is race, class, and gender that stops them from being appreciated. Either way, they continue to do what is suitable for children. I applaud your efforts.

Paycheck Collectors

There are several positive staff members, but there are staff members whom students should avoid. I call the latter paycheck collectors. Such teachers only care about their union rights and pension. They clock in, clock out, and vacate the community quickly. "Educators" uninterested in transforming lives should never work in urban schools. Children know the difference between educators and people who happen to work in a school building. Teachers have blatantly said, "I am here to teach, nothing else." What is more disgusting than teachers being indifferent about transforming the lives of Black children are closet racists. For example, a Black family has filed a claim against the Palmdale School District in California, alleging that a teacher went on a racist rant about them on Zoom earlier this year, apparently not knowing they were still listening (Romero et al., 2021). Unfortunately, there are more teachers like this in schools than the media likes to report. Such teachers should go to private schools, where social-emotional, cultural awareness isn't as necessary. But even there, revolutionary educators are needed. As the nation's racial tensions intensify, schools need bold educators prepared to transform lives.

12TH GRADE

Most 12th graders are under the assumption that they are already adults. Because of their surroundings, many teens act like adults. They face challenges that would break most. I'm amazed at high school seniors juggling multiple responsibilities and doing well academically. For example, Tupac Mosley, a Memphis high school senior, maintained a 4.3 GPA, scored a 31 on his ACT, and was chosen valedictorian—all while dealing with his father's death and the absence of a stable home. His achievements earned him a slew of college scholarships totaling more than $3 million (Kinder, 2019). Though his story is phenomenal, it shouldn't be the norm. Numerous Black students dream of college, of being independent, but have no resources. They are forced to help their parents financially. Internally, they contemplate having to go away to college when their parents are on welfare and have to face the devastation of drugs and living in a crime-ridden neighborhood. Guilt clouds their judgment, and many never attend college. Instead, they find minimum wage jobs in which they get stuck for decades. Initially, they feel that they can purchase the newest Yeezys, a fake chain, and a hoopty. Eventually, they become stuck, and going to college seems unreal.

A former student used to rave about the prospect of going to an HBCU (historically Black college or university). He was a great student, rarely had trouble in school, and came from a great family. He contacted a tuition assistance program for students from poor communities. He visited several HBCU campuses, but Morehouse called his name. He was interested in the majors offered. He attended the early college program and did well. After the summer program, he spoke of the campus and being happy about the school. Being in the presence of Black excellence impacted him. He was surrounded by like-minded people preparing to change the world. In the fall, he went back and continued on his journey. Classes were going well, and he was relishing being away from New York. Unfortunately, the program manager had a problem with my student, which led to the student losing his tuition support.

Supposedly, the manager used his influence to manipulate students into having sexual relationships. As a result of the conflict, the manager pulled the funds, and my former student was in debt for $20,000. His transcripts were held, he couldn't transfer, and he eventually began working at a local store. He is presently trying to get transcripts from Morehouse to apply to another school. He's on the brink of quitting because he doesn't see the sense of fighting so hard, with few results. High school seniors should realize that graduating doesn't lead to immediate financial stability. Afterward, they have to deal with increased debt from college tuition.

Delayed Gratification

Delaying gratification, rather than selecting an immediate reward, is widely regarded as an indication that a child is well adjusted or has high self-regulation skills (Duran & Grissmer, 2020). For Black children from diverse socioeconomic environments, the process and results are complex. Teaching youngsters how to delay instant pleasure, invest in future endeavors, and attend college is challenging. Black students have immediate primary needs that need close observation. Understanding how education incrementally leads to financial security is an obscure notion. As a teen, it was difficult to understand how completing algebra homework would put food on my mother's table. The great equalizer of education should be clearly explained to our children. To be precise, alternate forms of success such as entrepreneurship and trades are also options to a career path. Education has been the most used conduit for Black people. Students understanding the long-term process of how education transforms into capital increases the ability to be patient. Delayed gratification is something that all children should learn at all ages. Parents send a mixed message when repeatedly purchasing material items for their children. Hearing the word "no" is a foreign concept. Faster cell phones, social media, and the like conditions children to assume instant satisfaction. Their character is further compromised from living in a society focused on immediate gratification.

In high school, friends who were boosters and local drug dealers had the newest clothes; both groups seemed content. On the other hand, I wore the corniest clothes, avoided gangs, and ate free lunch. To avoid the extremes of being broke or being a drug dealer, students need to work part-time jobs. Expecting children to be filled with joy and happiness about academics is irrational. They are human beings with a range of interests, perspectives, and emotions. They live in a social media–driven world that discourages the importance of self-love. Twitter, TikTok, and Instagram are dictating how our children value themselves. Simultaneously, the platforms mentioned above are entertaining. Balance is key. Employment provides the opportunity to enjoy material items while learning financial independence.

Their Expectations about College

Twelfth graders have gross misconceptions of college: everyone has to graduate in four years, there is little financial support, and keeping a specific major are just a few of the nonsensical myths about college life (Knight Randolph, 2021). These untruths lead several Black students to avoid attending college. Their decision has severe consequences they are unable to fully comprehend in the moment. As teens living at home, their parents/guardians did most of the heavy lifting. In college, that comfort is gone, and independence is a mandate. Excessively coddled children struggle mightily, while others have a smoother conversion.

Completing college applications, paying specific bills, and opening accounts help improve independence. Parents who take over the tasks as mentioned above harm young adult children.

Parents and educators must do more than take Black children on a few college tours each year. They need to spend an extended amount of time discussing what to expect in college. Students need mentors who are presently college students to provide guidance. Also, educators must stop forcing students to go away to school, for there are many students who still have responsibilities at home. Living in a dorm would be great, but that is not a financially wise decision for most students.

When Students Are Independent

One significant advantage of increasing child independence is that youngsters learn how to aid those around them. In addition, you may help your child acquire confidence by providing them with activities that allow them to be more independent. You assist children in developing virtues such as patience, concentration, self-help, cooperation, self-discipline, and self-trust while teaching them new abilities (First Discoverers, 2017). Also, they think critically about each decision. Schools aren't designed to enhance decision-making skills. Schools create façades that misinform seniors. In school, when they come late, they receive a phone call home. When fighting, students are suspended and then readmitted. Lack of accountability jades their understanding of the world, and as adults, they lack basic professional skills. Real-life experiences quickly improve their skills. I've seen students on the brink of dropping out of school obtain part-time jobs, and ultimately change. A former student had trouble from the time she walked in the door. She smelled of marijuana daily, got into fights with other students, and cursed out teachers regularly. As a senior, she changed dramatically. She seldom got into trouble and was preparing to graduate on time. When I asked what made her change, she said, "I'm working at McDonald's, and I stopped hanging with certain friends."

FAKE FRIENDS

Tony Robbins's mentor, motivational speaker Jim Rohn, states that you are the average of the five people you spend the most time with. Jim Rohn is a world-renowned entrepreneur and author. Similarly, author and entrepreneur Tim Ferriss has riffed on this, saying, "You are the average of the five people you most associate with" (Shontell & Kane, 2017). In the 12th grade, many students have already critically analyzed friendships and made necessary adjustments according to their life goals. Pragmatic relationships replace superficial bonds. "Cool" kids realize they need help from "nerds." There is a realistic expectation that relationships must be equally resourceful. Teens have to parent their children or take care of siblings. Peer relationships have a deeper meaning as friends become family.

From freshman to senior year, tribes fully transition. Standing in the cafeteria, I have seen best friends become strangers. Each 9th-grade cohort morphs as students drop out, get left back, join gangs, and so on. When I walk into the 12th-grade lunchroom, what is usually left are nerds, artsy kids, and a straggling group of former cool kids trying to catch up. The popular group is scattered and attaches themselves to other groups. Nerds and artsy groups accept former cool kids trying to repent for their sins. Cool kids now need help from students whom they once ostracized. The new friendship is mutually beneficial, as nerds are more confident in academic accomplishments and cool kids are humbler.

As a senior, I was the formally cool kid who needed to find a new crew. My new friends weren't nerds per se. They were intelligent, hardworking, responsible, and consistent. All of the things that I was not. I felt uncomfortable acting out in their presence because I stuck out like a sore thumb. They held me accountable and had no problem correcting me. They would discuss upcoming exams, complete homework, and remind one another to study. Arrogantly, I hated knowing I had to rely on others. Eventually, I put my pride aside and accepted their mentoring. In every job, I do the same thing. Whoever is more intelligent or better at a task than I am, I make a friend. Doing so has done me well as an educational leader.

Peer mentorship programs have a favorable impact on student graduation rates, particularly among Black students (Sprague, 2007). Unfortunately, cultural norms have negatively influenced our understanding of peer mentoring. Black children are told not to ask for help from others. To some extent, I understand being mindful of being too vulnerable because specific communities demand exuding toughness. Not doing so can be fatal. Students want help from peers but are teased for doing so. Students should develop trusting, mutually beneficial relationships that support their academic growth.

Parents play a crucial role in training 12th graders to develop healthy peer relationships. If students are taught antisocial behaviors throughout their life, they will have difficulty creating healthy relationships. For example, being told to fight or stay away from all "fake" people leads to social issues. Students also imitate the ways that their parents maintain friendships. As parents, we have to model expectations, especially when it comes to our peers.

Family

Parental guidance must change in content and delivery to meet the learning needs of seniors in high school. Adults should avoid speaking to high school seniors like infantile children. Some Black parents have interesting rules about how children should speak. We say things like, "Do as I say, not as I do," "Mind your business," and "Because I said so." Such nearsighted hypocritical language has no power. Reflective conversations train children to be independent thinkers. Many youngsters are having sex, bearing children, and working around adults regularly. They are well informed and aren't intimidated by empty threats. Give them space to lead conversations and make their own decisions.

I remember a parent who would pack their 12th grader's lunch and visit the school regularly. It sounds nice at the beginning but becomes debilitating. Another former student was being raised by an overbearing single mother. The student was quiet and did well in school. Her mother was a bit older and yelled at the entire staff about anything. I tried having conversations with the mother about specific issues, and it never ended well. One afternoon this student was crying in the hall by my office. I asked what was happening, and she said, "I want to speak with my mom about my boyfriend, but I am afraid." She and her boyfriend would usually cut class to see each other in the halls. I would also have to redirect them back to class. I chose not to speak with her mother because I knew she would overreact for no reason. I told her that she would have to address her mother's overbearing behavior. She said, "I cannot wait to get out of the house to do whatever I want."

This example I just spoke of is happening to several high school seniors. If they are conditioned to avoid conflict at this age, how will they do in college? Helicopter parenting chases students away from home and toward danger. Most parents overact out of love and fear. They do not want their children to experience trauma in any way. After experiencing neglect and/or abuse and developing personal issues as children, parents make every effort to protect their children. Often the failed dreams of parents are projected onto their children. They overcompensate by being too rigid with their children. Ultimately, whether micromanaged or given total freedom, children make their own choices. Parents are responsible for helping them develop critical thinking skills that will positively guide those decisions. Don't be the parent who chases their child away after having them carry heavy, unrealistic burdens.

Bitter Teachers

Most of us will only retain grudges against a few people; others appear to acquire grudges quickly and vehemently. But, regardless of how they play out for you—and even if you don't consider yourself a "grudge-holding person," all of us have harbored a grudge at some point (Wilsner, 2018). The human condition holds for educators as well. Teachers' relationships with 12th graders come with a history. Teachers tend to resurface past issues with students. Throughout the years, some teachers keep records of wrongs to be used at an opportune moment. For example, one teacher enjoyed watching students whom she had conflicts with struggle to graduate. Her third marking period grades were her final revenge. She relished the power to force students to complete boring assignments to graduate on time. At first, I did not realize the pattern.

The teacher had no connection to students and horrible classroom management skills. Black boys had the most challenging time in her class. Her content was literacy, and the topics weren't culturally relevant. When students would be preparing to graduate in May, she would have a list of students she deemed "not ready to graduate." Without fail, the reason she failed them was homework. Students would complain about favoritism in the classroom. From my experience, teachers have subtle ways of belittling children in classrooms and acting innocent when the student reacts. All it takes is a witty remark, a smirk, and so forth. When students complain about a teacher, I do not automatically disregard their claims.

I dreaded meeting with this person. The privilege and arrogance seeped through her pores and corroded her tongue. Our administrative team created grading policies to provide structure and advocate for the student. Students would buckle down and complete missing assignments toward the end of the marking period. Other students who couldn't stand the teacher chose to cut class and go to summer school. I hated seeing students miss their graduation ceremony because of a biased teacher. Eventually, the teacher and I agreed her services were no longer needed in our school. She needed a private, specialized school and a leader who didn't look like me, someone she thought worthy of her respect. Thank God she left. We were able to hire more culturally relevant teachers from the community that improved student outcomes.

Social-Emotional Intelligence of Teachers

Social-emotional intelligence (SEI) is essential in all grades and especially important in the 12th grade. Young teachers tend to be better at SEI than older teachers. Understanding the lived experiences of Black children improves staff members' SEI exponentially. Educators from all races struggle with being sensitive to Black children. I have observed white, Black, Brown, Asian, and so forth teachers who are overly aggressive toward Black children. Some Black teachers abandon their identity, trying to be recognized by the administration. The fear of seeming lazy pushes many Black educators to become unnecessarily harsh. Our children need people willing to lighten up and have a little fun with students.

FUN STUFF

School Trips

Senior activities are one of the best parts of high school. You have the opportunity to share unforgettable moments with lifelong friends. I still look at my old pictures from senior prom and graduation. At the time, I was too poor for the senior trip. As a teacher/administrator, I have gone to a couple. Seeing inner-city students in nature is the best. For a short time, they get to breathe fresh air and relax. Presently, we have an annual Florida trip that my veteran teachers facilitate. I haven't gone yet, being that I want my first experience to be with biological children. Students come back excited and grateful for the occasion.

Proms ARE LIT

The senior prom is always a huge event. Seniors go over the top trying to buy the most expensive dresses, tuxedoes, jewelry, et cetera. Yet, every year I see students transform their entire appearance and personality for that one day. In communities I've worked in, the whole community participates. No matter how much a student has struggled in school, they are on top of the world for that one day. These pictures stay in the students' mental Rolodexes for their entire life. People still tell stories about prom decades later.

My favorite part of prom is seeing people who were unpopular transform. When they take the time to do their hair and get new clothes, everyone is super excited. We usually have one of the "popular" girls ask a not so "popular" boy to the prom and vice versa. Unfortunately, my students often cut school to prepare the party. I tell the gentlemen to ease up and not be too aggressive with the outfits. The spotlight should be for the ladies. There is always one guy who tries to do too much and ends up embarrassing them.

My prom was one to remember. We felt like superstars in the hood. Kids ran behind the limousine, and all the gangsters gave us props. In Brownsville, when high school students come through for prom, all tensions dissipate. People who barely acknowledge your existence open their hearts for a moment to show a little love. Driving through New York City screaming out of the top of a limo is a teenager's dream. We felt like Nas and Lauryn Hill. "If I Ruled the World" by Nas was hot back then, so it was appropriate. We made up this dumb crew name, Boss Players. A handshake developed, and we threw up finger signs to seal the deal. Proms are memorable moments that stick with you for a lifetime. Probably that is why I remember every detail twenty-five years later. A quick note to the parents: do not go bankrupt as much as you want your child to be happy. I've seen parents struggling on welfare purchase thousand-dollar dresses. Purchase what you can and just let them be kids for one last time.

Once we got into the party, we had so much fun. Everyone danced. This is before Facebook and Instagram desocialized children. Dating myself here, we rocked out to Big, Nas, Onyx, Wu, Fugees, Mary J., and the bogle riddim. My friend Seneca had too much to drink and vomited; Courtney took small vampire nibbles on some girl's arms. High school sweethearts broke up, and new couples emerged. For my fashion efforts, I won the prom prince alongside my friend Wilfredo. He was hands down the best dressed, so I didn't feel upset. The night ended on Coney Island beach, taking Boss Player pictures and cracking jokes.

Educators and parents must make these moments memorable for our students. As an administrator, I have seen students who never got recognition enjoy themselves with their peers. Sadly, for some students, this will be the last time they graduate from an educational institution. Therefore, this moment is significant. I encourage staff members to get dressed up and enjoy themselves as well. We have been pointing out the students' shortcomings at every turn. However, we must also be present to celebrate their accomplishments. I have seen staff members complain about students every day and then when it's time to celebrate their achievements: silence. The subtle message to students is, "I never cared about your happiness or joy."

However, parents must be careful not to overdo this celebration. You do not want your child thinking this is the end of their educational journey. Save some of your money for their college application, books, and so forth. This is also an excellent time for parents to set aside their differences and support their children collaboratively. You don't want to use this time to air your grievances toward each other. If you're separated, be clear with the person you are dating about your expectations as well. There shouldn't be stepparents or significant others using this moment to prove a point.

GRADUATION: END OF THE ROAD

Graduation is the best part of the whole experience. Students and parents are filled with joy. The sense of accomplishment radiates through all the family members. Everyone takes pride in helping the young person succeed. The uncle who cut hair and the grandmother who babysat all feel the same level of joy. As a principal, I have to argue with families at most ceremonies. People try sneaking in. Being the softie that I am, I let them in. I understand the importance of the moment. The parents' tears of joy are a beautiful thing to watch. Tough exteriors are shattered with strong emotions. Seeing their baby girl/boy walk across the stage melts their hearts.

Educators feel the same amount of pride. Seeing a student who gave you headaches for four years finally finish is a sense of validation like no other. I usually cry at these events like a baby. I try to hold it in, but then I remember the stories of the students walking past me. Students who triumphed over insurmountable obstacles all move me to tears. Handshakes from grandparents with spider veins and arthritis remind me of my purpose, my why.

REMEMBER YOUR WHY

Educators, remember your purpose. You may not receive the recognition of high-performing schools. Working in an urban school filled with minority students isn't for the faint of heart. Your reward will never be outward adoration. I've come to realize that this work is a calling, not a job. The constant fights with administrators, students, and parents can be overwhelming. Working in "easier" schools is tempting. Logically speaking, why would anyone choose unnecessary stress? The simple answer is love. We love our students, we love what we do, and we love working in schools where we are needed. Do not waste your talents in schools where the students barely need you. Work in schools that will transform your core values and push you to be your best self. Being at graduation with your students feels like winning the lottery.

In all honesty, not all stories end positively, though. Some students do not graduate on time. I hate having to tell their parents. I blame myself, the staff, and the educational system for failing them. Others point to the student's lack of desire and other excuses to avoid admitting failure. A few come back for summer school, while others transfer to adult education programs to finish. Several students drop out, get jobs at local stores, drive Ubers, and work at temp agencies. It's challenging to convince them to go back to school once life starts taking over. They have children, develop vices, and lose interest. But, as a school leader, I feel entirely responsible and try in every way to convince them to go back.

Then some students lose their lives from getting involved in the wrong crowd. Recently a student very near and dear to my heart was murdered in cold blood. I used to cut his hair; I bought him sandwiches (bacon, egg, and cheese), sneakers, and clothes when he needed them. He would come to my office and tell me about his problems in the street. He was tough and could fight with anyone. His brother was killed a few years before him by a rival gang as well. They didn't want to fight Shaheem because he was a good boxer. When he cut class, I chased him out of the halls and told him, "I love you" every time I saw him. He was like a son to me. He didn't graduate on time, but the school's guidance counselor and I continued to reach out to him. I pleaded and pleaded with him to leave the gang life. It didn't work.

Early this year (2021), I was told Shaheem was murdered somewhere in East New York off Linden Avenue. What made it worse was that his last moments were caught on camera. Someone sent a recording on the Citizen app. He could be seen gasping for air while lying on the concrete next to the housing projects. Word has it that a female set him up on a virtual dating app. He was ambushed and shot several times in the upper torso. At nineteen years old, his life began to leave his body while someone stood on the side recording it. The police officers on the scene tried everything they could. His Afro was sticking out of his hoodie and bubble goose-down jacket. I cannot get the image out of my head even now. After doctors at a local hospital tried their best, he was gone. Shaheem Bascom.

Early in my career, the same thing happened to another student, Shaquille Jones. I was working at South Shore High School. He was another one who stayed in my office for free cuts, McDonald's, and to play basketball after school. His smile could light up a room. Always up to no good, he was misunderstood by most people. The tough-guy act never worked with me. I could always get him to laugh and settle down in class. Unfortunately, a situation with rival schools with differing gang affiliations led to his death. Someone rushed in while he was cutting class in McDonald's on Flatlands across the street from the school. A chase ensued, and Shaquille was struck by gunfire. I would always tell him to put a belt on and pull up his pants. A news article showed his lifeless body lying on the ground. When looking closer, you could see his pants sagging, and his Polo boots were untied. He tripped and was caught in an alley off of Flatlands.

When I heard the news, I cried. I felt guilty and responsible. I'd just left South Shore to become a principal at my current school. "If I were there, probably I could have kept him in my office for a cut," I told myself. Guilt led me to get into a car crash. He came to me a dream that evening as well. Both students also pushed me to write this book.

Shaheem, Shaquille, Darren, and Nicholas, this was for you. I hope I made you proud.

References

Afro-Latino Report. (2016, February 29). *How U.S. Afro-Latinos report their race*. Pew Research Center. https://www.pewresearch.org/wp-content/uploads/2016/02/FT_16.02.22_afroLatino_race_310px.png

Alsubaie, M. A. (2015). Hidden curriculum as one of current issue of curriculum. *Journal of Education and Practice, 6*(33), 125–128.

Anderson, J. (2015, November 26). *Parents: Your absurdly high expectations are harming your children's achievement*. Quartz. https://qz.com/559821/parents-your-absurdly-high-expectations-are-harming-your-childrens-achievement/

Anderson, J. D. (1988). *The education of Blacks in the South, 1860–1935* (New edition). University of North Carolina Press.

Ba, A. U. (2016). Cost of growing up in dysfunctional family. *Journal of Family Medicine and Disease Prevention*. https://clinmedjournals.org/articles/jfmdp/journal-of-family-medicine-and-disease-prevention-jfmdp-3-059.php?jid=jfmdp

Barnhart, T. (2021, September 15). Mom arrested for alleged fight with 11-year-old student on school bus. *Newsweek*. https://www.newsweek.com/mom-arrested-alleged-fight-11-year-old-student-school-bus-1629621

Barnum, M. (2018, March 23). *Race, not just poverty, shapes who graduates in America—and other education lessons from a big new study*. Chalkbeat. https://chalkbeat.org/posts/us/2018/03/23/race-not-just-poverty-shapes-who-graduates-in-america-and-other-education-lessons-from-a-big-new-study/

Bell, D. A. (1993). *Faces at the bottom of the well: The permanence of racism*. Basic Books. https://www.amazon.com/Faces-At-Bottom-Well-Permanence/dp/0465068146

Bidwell, C. R., & Stinson, D. W. (2016). *Crossing "the problem of the color line": White mathematics teachers and Black students*. North American Chapter of the International Group for the Psychology of Mathematics Education. https://eric.ed.gov/?q=teacher+student+relationships+outcomes+achievement+success+African-American+Black&pr=on&ft=on&ff1=subTeacher+Student+Relationship&ff2=pubReports+-+Research&pg=2&id=ED583795

Brennan, D. (2021, August 18). *Why does teenage rebellion happen?* MedicineNet. https://www.medicinenet.com/why_does_teenage_rebellion_happen/article.htm

Burnett, G., & Walz, G. (1994). *Gangs in the schools*. ERIC Digest 99. https://eric.ed.gov/?id=ED372175

Carr, A. (2014). The evidence base for family therapy and systemic interventions for child-focused problems. *Journal of Family Therapy, 36*(2), 107–157. https://doi.org/10.1111/1467-6427.12032

Cherry, K. (2021, April 7). *Why do we dream?* Verywell Mind. https://www.verywellmind.com/why-do-we-dream-top-dream-theories-2795931

Crabbe, R., Pivnick, L. K., Bates, J., Gordon, R. A., & Crosnoe, R. (2019). Contemporary college students' reflections on their high school peer crowds. *Journal of Adolescent Research, 34*(5), 563–596. https://doi.org/10.1177/0743558418809537

Desiraju, M. (2021). *Your child's growth (for parents)*. Nemours Kidshealth. https://kidshealth.org/en/parents/childs-growth.html

Duran, C. A. K., & Grissmer, D. W. (2020). Choosing immediate over delayed gratification correlates with better school-related outcomes in a sample of children of color from low-income families. *Developmental Psychology, 56*(6), 1107–1120. https://doi.org/10.1037/dev0000920

Family Education. (2021, September 17). *Teaching your child to protect himself*. https://www.familyeducation.com/life/physical-sexual-abuse/teaching-your-child-protect-himself

Ferguson, A. A. (2001). *Bad boys: Public schools in the making of Black masculinity*. University of Michigan Press.

Fine, M. (1991). *Framing dropouts*. SUNY Series, Teacher Empowerment and School Reform. https://www.sunypress.edu/p-958-framing-dropouts.aspx

First Discoverers. (2017, August 21). Why child independence is important. https://www.firstdiscoverers.co.uk/encouraging-child-independence/

Freire, P., & Macedo, D. (2018). *Pedagogy of the oppressed: 50th anniversary edition* (4th ed.). Bloomsbury Academic.

Gates, H. L., & Root, J. (2013, January 10). "The talented tenth" origins. *The African Americans: Many Rivers to Cross* (African American History Blog). https://www.pbs.org/wnet/african-americans-many-rivers-to-cross/history/who-really-invented-the-talented-tenth/

Gibson, P. A., Wilson, R., Haight, W., Kayama, M., & Marshall, J. M. (2014). The role of race in the out-of-school suspensions of Black students: The perspectives of students with suspensions, their parents and educators. *Children and Youth Services Review, 47*, 274–282. https://doi.org/10.1016/j.childyouth.2014.09.020

Gill, B., & Lerner, J. (2017, January 25). Here's what works for teacher accountability. *Education Week*. https://www.edweek.org/teaching-learning/opinion-heres-what-works-for-teacher-accountability/2017/01

Gordon, D. M., Iwamoto, D., Ward, N., Potts, R., & Boyd, E. (2009). Mentoring urban Black middle-school male students: Implications for academic achievement. *Journal of Negro Education, 78*(3), 277–289.

Greenidge, K. (2019, April 9). Why Black people discriminate among ourselves: The toxic legacy of colorism. *The Guardian*. https://www.theguardian.com/lifeandstyle/2019/apr/09/colorism-racism-why-black-people-discriminate-among-ourselves

Hickman, C. B. (1997). The devil and the one drop rule: Racial categories, African Americans, and the U.S. Census. *Michigan Law Review*, *95*(5), 1161. https://doi.org/10.2307/1290008

Holloman, L. O., LaPoint, V., Alleyne, S. I., Palmer, R. J., & Sanders-Phillips, K. (1996). Dress-related behavioral problems and violence in the public school setting: Prevention, intervention, and policy—A holistic approach. *Journal of Negro Education*, *65*(3), 267–281. https://doi.org/10.2307/2967344

Hunter, A. G., Chipenda-Dansokho, S., Tarver, S. Z., Herring, M., & Fletcher, A. (2019). Social capital, parenting, and African American families. *Journal of Child and Family Studies*, *28*(2), 547–559. https://doi.org/10.1007/s10826-018-1282-2

Hyman, I. A. (1989, April 26). The "make-believe world" of *Lean on Me*. *Education Week*. https://www.edweek.org/education/opinion-the-make-believe-world-of-lean-on-me/1989/04

Jackson, A. P. (1999). The effects of nonresident father involvement on single Black mothers and their young children. *Social Work*, *44*(2), 156–166. https://doi.org/10.1093/sw/44.2.156

Joiner, L. (2016, April 19). *Hurt: The impact of father-absence on the mental health of Black boys*. Center for Health Journalism. https://centerforhealthjournalism.org/fellowships/projects/hurt-impact-father-absence-mental-health-black-boys

Juvenile Violent Crime. (2021). *Juvenile violent crime: Time of day (offenders per 1,000 juvenile violent crime offenders)*. https://www.ojjdp.gov/ojstatbb/offenders/qa03301.asp

Kendrick, C. (2021). *Parents have unrealistic academic expectations*. FamilyEducation. https://www.familyeducation.com/life/motivation/parents-have-unrealistic-academic-expectations

Kennedy, R. (2001). Racial passing. *Ohio State Law Journal*, *62*.

Kenyatta, C. P. (2012). From perception to practice: How teacher-student interactions affect African American male achievement. *Journal of Urban Learning, Teaching, and Research*, *8*, 36–44.

Kinder, G. (2019, May 22). *Homeless valedictorian scores more than $3 million in college scholarships*. CNN. https://www.cnn.com/2019/05/22/us/homeless-valedictorian-scholarship-millions-trnd/index.html

Knight Randolph, K. (2021, February 24). *10 completely false college myths*. Fastweb. https://www.fastweb.com/college-search/articles/the-10-completely-false-college-myths

Kozol, J. (1985). *Death at an early age: The classic indictment of inner-city education*. Plume. https://www.amazon.com/Death-Early-Age-Indictment-Inner-City/dp/0452262925

Kukuk, D. (2019, April 1). *Whittle: Support staff are backbone of our schools*. AFT Michigan. https://aftmichigan.org/whittle-support-staff-are-backbone-of-our-schools/

Ladson-Billings, G. J. (2007). *Association toward a theory of culturally relevant pedagogy*.

Laninga-Wijnen, L., Harakeh, Z., Garandeau, C. F., Dijkstra, J. K., Veenstra, R., & Vollebergh, W. A. M. (2019). Classroom popularity hierarchy predicts prosocial and aggressive popularity norms across the school year. *Child Development*, *90*(5), e637–e653. https://doi.org/10.1111/cdev.13228

Leary, J. D. (2004). *Post traumatic slave syndrome*. Uptone Press.

Lebert-Charron, A., Dorard, G., Boujut, E., & Wendland, J. (2018). Maternal burnout syndrome: Contextual and psychological associated factors. *Frontiers in Psychology*, *9*, 885. https://doi.org/10.3389/fpsyg.2018.00885

Lee, K. (2021, February 25). *Why too much cell phone usage can hurt your family relationships*. Verywell Family. https://www.verywellfamily.com/negative-effects-of-too-much-cell-phone-use-621152

Leibowitz, B. (2011, April 8). *N.J. teacher caught in lie loses two jobs, and credentials*. CBS. https://www.cbsnews.com/news/nj-teacher-caught-in-lie-loses-two-jobs-and-credentials/

Loewus, L. (2017, August 23). The nation's teaching force is still mostly white and female. *Education Week*. https://www.edweek.org/ew/articles/2017/08/15/the-nations-teaching-force-is-still-mostly.html

Mackin, J. J. (2014, January 1). 2014 resolution: Stop watching feel-good teacher movies. *The Atlantic*. https://www.theatlantic.com/education/archive/2014/01/2014-resolution-stop-watching-feel-good-teacher-movies/282741/

Malsen, P. (2015, December 29). *The social and academic benefits of team sports*. Edutopia. https://www.edutopia.org/discussion/social-and-academic-benefits-team-sports

Martin, E. P., & Mitchell, J. (1982). *The Black extended family*. University of Chicago Press. https://press.uchicago.edu/ucp/books/book/chicago/B/bo28248639.html

McWhorter, J. (2019, July 20). The origins of the "acting white" charge. *The Atlantic*. https://www.theatlantic.com/ideas/archive/2019/07/acting-white-charge-origins/594130/

Meminger, D. (2020, September 14). *On the beat in Brownsville: Murders up more than 70%*. NY1 Spectrum News. https://www.ny1.com/nyc/all-boroughs/public-safety/2020/09/13/on-the-beat-in-brownsville--murders-up-more-than-70-

Miller, E. (2021, March 1). *For some Black students, remote learning has offered a chance to thrive*. NPR. https://www.npr.org/2021/03/01/963282430/for-some-black-students-remote-learning-has-offered-a-chance-to-thrive

Montgomery, E., Just-Østergaard, E., & Jervelund, S. S. (2019). Transmitting trauma: A systematic review of the risk of child abuse perpetrated by parents exposed to traumatic events. *International Journal of Public Health*, *64*(2), 241–251. https://doi.org/10.1007/s00038-018-1185-4

Neal, M. A. (2018, June 15). Opinion: Black fathers and the shame of absenteeism. *Durham Herald Sun*. https://www.heraldsun.com/opinion/article213260719.html

Nelsen, J. (1985). The three r's of logical consequences, the three r's of punishment, and the six steps for winning children over. *Individual Psychology*, *41*(2), 161. ProQuest. https://www.proquest.com/openview/60c677b0d2433dba31b13b230d0e316c/1?pq-origsite=gscholar&cbl=1816606

Nguyen, A. W., Chatters, L. M., & Taylor, R. J. (2016). African American extended family and church-based social network typologies. *Family Relations*, *65*(5), 701–715. https://doi.org/10.1111/fare.12218

Novotney, A. (2010, October). *The power of Dad.* American Psychological Association. https://www.apa.org/monitor/2010/10/dad

NYS Student Report. (2021). *NY State—Student and educator report (2017–18).* NYSED Data Site. https://data.nysed.gov/studenteducator.php

Okonofua, B. A. (2013). "I am Blacker than you": Theorizing conflict between African immigrants and African Americans in the United States. *SAGE Open, 3*(3), 2158244013499162. https://doi.org/10.1177/2158244013499162

Onetti, W., Fernández-García, J. C., & Castillo-Rodríguez, A. (2019). Transition to middle school: Self-concept changes. *PLoS ONE, 14*(2), e0212640. https://doi.org/10.1371/journal.pone.0212640

Parke, R., & Clarke-Stewart, K. A. (2002). *Effects of parental incarceration on young children* [Paper presentation]. From Prison to Home Conference. 20.

Patton, S. (2014, September 20). *Understanding Black America and the spanking debate.* BBC News. https://www.bbc.com/news/magazine-29261462

Phipps, A. (2021). White tears, white rage: Victimhood and (as) violence in mainstream feminism. *European Journal of Cultural Studies, 24*(1), 81–93. https://doi.org/10.1177/1367549420985852

Pilgrim, D. (2014). *Brown paper bag test: February 2014 question of the month.* Jim Crow Museum, Ferris State University. https://www.ferris.edu/HTMLS/news/jimcrow/question/2014/february.htm

Podoshen, J. S., Andrzejewski, S. A., & Hunt, J. M. (2014). Materialism, conspicuous consumption, and American hip-hop subculture. *Journal of International Consumer Marketing, 26*(4), 271–283. https://doi.org/10.1080/08961530.2014.900469

Roberson, J. (2019, July 11). *A Black counternarrative.* Public Books. https://www.publicbooks.org/a-black-counternarrative/

Roberts, K. (2014, June 15). *When parents lie.* Psychology Today. https://www.psychologytoday.com/us/blog/savvy-parenting/201406/when-parents-lie

Roberts, N. (2019, April 14). *"Get your hands off me": Security officers investigated after video shows them assault a black student.* NewsOne. https://newsone.com/3850898/columbia-barnard-college-racial-profiling-video/

Romero, L., Saucedo, C., & Salahieh, N. (2021, March 26). *Teacher's caught-on-video racist rant leads Black family to file claim against Palmdale School District.* KTLA. https://ktla.com/news/local-news/teachers-caught-on-video-racist-rant-leads-black-family-to-file-claim-against-palmdale-school-district/

Saunders, J. A., Davis, L., Williams, T. D., & Williams, J. H. (2004). Gender differences in self-perceptions and academic outcomes: A study of African American high school students. *Journal of Youth and Adolescence, 30*, 81–90.

Scheidegger, J. (2019, September 12). *New survey highlights disconnect between high school and the real world.* Kauffman Foundation. https://www.kauffman.org/currents/new-survey-highlights-disconnect-between-high-school-and-real-world/

Sesin, C. (2020, September 4). *Trump cultivated the Latino vote in Florida, and it paid off.* NBC News. https://www.nbcnews.com/news/latino/trump-cultivated-latino-vote-florida-it-paid-n1246226

Seymour, S. C. (2013). "It takes a village to raise a child": Attachment theory and multiple child care in Alor, Indonesia, and in North India. In N. Quinn & J. M. Mageo (Eds.), *Attachment reconsidered: Cultural perspectives on a Western theory* (pp. 115–139). Palgrave Macmillan US. https://doi.org/10.1057/9781137386724_5

Shontell, A., & Kane, L. (2017, May 7). *The CEO of a multimillion-dollar company explains why you should dump your "loser" friends.* Business Insider. https://www.businessinsider.com/gary-vaynerchuk-audit-friends-2017-5

Sirota, M. (2017, February 27). *Spoiling your teen is ruining their life.* HuffPost. https://www.huffingtonpost.ca/marcia-sirota/teenagers-and-entitlement_b_15010970.html

Smith, C. (1993). *How can parents model good listening skills?* ERIC. https://eric.ed.gov/?id=ED376481

Smith, C. (2021, June 20). *Comedian Amber Ruffin exposes history of Black towns being flooded for lakes and parks in viral clip.* BIN: Black Information Network. https://www.binnews.com/content/2021-06-30-amber-ruffin-exposes-history-of-flooding-black-towns-in-viral-clip/

Sprague, C. K. (2007). *The impact of peer mentoring on the academic and nonacademic performance of high school students* [Doctoral dissertation, Seton Hall University]. Seton Hall University Dissertations and Theses (ETDs). 156. https://scholarship.shu.edu/dissertations/1595/?utm_source=scholarship.shu.edu%2Fdissertations%2F1595&utm_medium=PDF&utm_campaign=PDFCoverPages

Tan, C. Y., Lyu, M., & Peng, B. (2020). Academic benefits from parental involvement are stratified by parental socioeconomic status: A meta-analysis. *Parenting, 20*(4), 241–287. https://doi.org/10.1080/15295192.2019.1694836

Tatum, B. D. (2017). *"Why are all the Black kids sitting together in the cafeteria?" And other conversations about race* (Revised and updated). Basic Books.

Terada, Y. (2021, March 26). *Why Black teachers walk away.* Edutopia. https://www.edutopia.org/article/why-black-teachers-walk-away

Thomas, A. (2017, April). *Promoting culturally affirming parenting in African-American parents.* American Psychological Association. https://www.apa.org/pi/families/resources/newsletter/2017/04/african-american-parents

Threlfall, J. M., Seay, K. D., & Kohl, P. L. (2013). The parenting role of African American fathers in the context of urban poverty. *Journal of Children & Poverty, 19*(1), 45–61. https://doi.org/10.1080/10796126.2013.764846

Toshalis, E. (2015). *Make me! Understanding and engaging student resistance in school* (Illustrated edition). Harvard Education Press.

Trousdale, A. M. (1990). A submission theology for Black Americans: Religion and social action in prize-winning children's books about the Black experience in America. *Research in the Teaching of English, 24*(2), 117–140.

Tyng, C. M., Amin, H. U., Saad, M. N. M., & Malik, A. S. (2017). The influences of emotion on learning and memory. *Frontiers in Psychology, 8*, 1454. https://doi.org/10.3389/fpsyg.2017.01454

Wallace, B. K. (2017, February 8). *When it comes to school, harsh parenting can backfire.* CNN. https://www.cnn.com/2017/02/08/health/harsh-parenting-education-study/index.html

Whitfield, C. (2019, January 29). *Only two percent of teachers are Black men, yet research confirms they matter*. KIPP Public Charter Schools. https://www.kipp.org/news/two-percent-teachers-black-men-yet-research-confirms-matter/

Wilder, S. (2014). Effects of parental involvement on academic achievement: A meta-synthesis. *Educational Review, 66*(3), 377–397. https://doi.org/10.1080/00131911.2013.780009

Wilkerson, I. (2020). *Caste: The origins of our discontents*. Random House.

Wilsner, W. (2018, December 6). *Here's the psychological reason we hold grudges*. Thrive Global. https://thriveglobal.com/stories/psychological-reason-hold-grudges/

Winten, M. (2018, May 10). "This Is America" by Childish Gambino explained. *Nolala*. https://www.nolala.com/en/current/an-analysis-of-the-meaning-of-the-lyrics-and-official-music-video-of-childish-gambino-this-is-america/

Young, Y. (2016, October 4). Teachers' implicit bias against Black students starts in preschool, study finds. *The Guardian*. https://www.theguardian.com/world/2016/oct/04/black-students-teachers-implicit-racial-bias-preschool-study

www.ingramcontent.com/pod-product-compliance
Lightning Source LLC
Chambersburg PA
CBHW030144240426
43672CB00005B/263